USER-DIRECTED COMPETITIVE INTELLIGENCE

USER-DIRECTED COMPETITIVE INTELLIGENCE

Closing the Gap Between Supply and Demand

WALTER D. BARNDT, JR.

QUORUM BOOKS
Westport, Connecticut • London

Library of Congress Cataloging-in-Publication Data

Barndt, Walter D.
    User-directed competitive intelligence : closing the gap between
supply and demand / Walter D. Barndt, Jr.
      p.   cm.
    Includes bibliographical references and index.
    ISBN 0–89930–781–7 (alk. paper)
    1. Business intelligence.   I. Title.
HD38.7.B37   1994
658.4′7—dc20   93–49030

British Library Cataloguing in Publication Data is available.

Library of Congress Catalog Card Number: 93–49030
ISBN: 0–89930–781–7

First published in 1994

Quorum Books, 88 Post Road West, Westport, CT 06881
An imprint of Greenwood Publishing Group, Inc.

Printed in the United States of America

The paper used in this book complies with the
Permanent Paper Standard issued by the National
Information Standards Organization (Z39.48–1984).

10 9 8 7 6 5 4 3 2 1

Contents

Foreword

Here is a parable to illustrate the degrees by which our nature may be enlightened or unenlightened.[1]

Thus begins Plato's analogy of the cave in his *Republic*.   In this book Professor Barndt has set out to explain the unexplainable to those who need to learn about intelligence, like the *prisoners* in the cave, and particularly those who need to learn how to use intelligence as a management discipline. This book is also for those practitioners who know that their organizations need intelligence and, in spite of an unreceptive audience, continue to produce the intelligence that they believe is necessary to protect their companies from competitive surprise and business failure.

The task, probably an impossible one, still needs to be attempted. Although both sides may recognize that the company needs better intelligence, it is doubtful that they understand or recognize the other side's key role and their interdependency in the intelligence game. Thus, Professor Barndt undertakes to resolve the production–demand dilemma that is, in many respects, closely paralleled by Plato's allegory of the cave.

The intelligence practitioner, the producer of intelligence, seems to have a basic urge to gather, analyze, and produce the intelligence, and, at the same time, the need to develop his or her skills and to further the profession's understanding of the intelligence process. The practitioner seems bent on helping the organization—whether it wants to be helped or not—to compete, to succeed, and in some cases, to survive. The Society of Competitive Intelligence Professionals (SCIP)[2] has provided a forum for these practitioners to learn, to develop, and to practice their skills. In the seven years since the Society was founded, the level of practitioner skills and understanding has grown to the point that the intelligence producers' ability to produce intelligence far outstrips senior management's understanding and capabilities to use that intelligence for the benefit of the company and for their own managerial enhancement.

Among users there is an ignorance, almost an arrogance, associated with competitive or business intelligence. Few executives have recognized the need for this new management tool, and fewer yet have adopted it and are practicing it with understanding and skill levels comparable to those of their government counterparts, the ambassadors, commanding generals, and national security policy-makers.

Arrogance or ignorance? Which is it that inhibits managers, whether they be American, or German, or Swedish, from recognizing this deficiency in their education and execution of their management duties? Contrasted with Japanese executives, who deeply value the library and the information sources from which business intelligence is derived, American managers seem to have turned their backs on such repositories of knowledge. Universities in North America and Europe do not teach intelligence as a management discipline. This may, in fact, be the basic reason for a lack of managerial appreciation of this set of skills. But what is the difference between Japanese and American managers that causes the Japanese to value intelligence about the competition and to seek all professional means of gathering and using it to the advantage and success of their enterprises?

In many instances, it is not so much managerial ignorance as arrogance. Most American and European leaders believe they have the competitive intelligence they need; or they can easily get it when they need it; or even, possibly, they believe that the information about their competitors that they receive *is* intelligence. Furthermore, some managers believe they do not need to know about the competition. Competitors do not seem to amount to much in their scheme of things—only the customer does. Alternatively, some executives assume that operational managers are responsible for getting the intelligence the company needs, and it is not their role to see that competitive intelligence is either collected or developed. In fact, they believe theirs is a higher responsibility, that of overseeing the company's image and ensuring that the company not only performs well financially but is perceived by the financial community as being a good investment. Of course, there are some cases in which corporate leaders honestly do not realize that intelligence is necessary—a sort of intellectual blind spot. In the final analysis, it seems that the user community within American companies is represented mainly by the ignorant when it comes to the creation or use of organized intelligence.

Professor Barndt has chosen to attack this situation on two fronts: the ignorance of both producers and users. If successful, the text that he has produced will meet the educational needs of both. This book provides basic insights for the practitioner to better understand the intelligence producer–user relationship, and it makes the case for the strong interdependence required for an organization to truly act intelligently as in Plato's cave. Plato describes education as not putting knowledge into a person who does not possess it but, rather, causing that person, who is looking in the wrong direction, to be turned the way he or she ought to be looking. "In the world of knowledge, the last thing to be perceived and only with great difficulty is the essential Form of Goodness."[3]

If successful, this book will meet the educational needs of both producers and users of intelligence, resulting in enlightened intelligent management for corporations. I believe that this effort has been a sincere attempt at that objective. Only the reader will know whether it has been successful.

Jan P. Herring

NOTES

1. William Ebenstein. *Great Political Thinkers.* New York: Rinehart, 1960. p. 55 (from *The Republic of Plato*, Oxford University Press, 1945)

2. Professor Barndt was recently elected to the Society's Board of Directors.

3. William Ebenstein. *Great Political Thinkers.*   New York: Rinehart, 1960. p. 57 (from *The Republic of Plato*, Oxford University Press, 1945)

Preface and Acknowledgments

In ten years of teaching, study, and participation in this new intelligence industry, I find I know less rather than more about all the issues, problems, and conditions of the industry; therefore, this book is incomplete. And while secondary research has been modest and primary research essentially nil, relevant research issues are emerging. While recognizing that much is still to be done, I am motivated to write now because I believe that the topic is important now and that intelligence is a key, if not the primary, potential source of competitive advantage for organizations in their efforts to sustain, grow, and profit from their investments and activities. Further, I believe that the competitive intelligence industry is on a dangerously flat growth plateau and will slip downward unless we aggressively seek ways to stimulate intelligence demand among organizational users. I look on this effort as only a start in the process of further developing competitive intelligence as a credible, reliable, valuable, and necessary user product.

I am grateful to many people, both inside and outside the competitive intelligence industry, for their insights, knowledge, and support for this endeavor. Jan Herring and Marshall Heyman have been enormously helpful in critiquing and stimulating my thinking and grasp of a theme and focus for the book.

Jan Herring, who contributed the foreword, is vice president of business planning and strategy at the Futures Group. After a distinguished career with the Central Intelligence Agency, he developed in the mid–1980s, the first comprehensive competitive intelligence system in the United States, at Motorola. Jan is widely recognized for his contributions to the development and growth of the competitive intelligence industry. He was recently selected as the recipient of the Society of Competitive Intelligence Professionals meritorious award. He also is a recipient of the medal of distinction and medal of merit from the CIA.

Marshall Heyman, who contributed Chapter 8 and a portion of Chapter 7, founded the Behavioral Assessment System Center in 1979 when he retired as chief psychologist (Operations) for the Central Intelligence Agency. He continues to serve national security interests as a consultant and lecturer to the U.S. military intelligence services, the FBI, and the Secret Service. He is an expert in psychological factors associated with high–stress activities and continues to devote much energy and enthusiasm to research, study, and publication.

Both men have made significant contributions—perhaps the most significant contributions—to this book. I am particularly grateful to them and to then president of the Hartford Graduate Center, Worth Loomis and the dean of the School of Management, William Luddy, for their encouraging support. For preparation of the numerous drafts and final manuscript and for so patiently coping with my uncertain handwriting skills, I wish to thank Elizabeth Barndt and Nancy Baker. Cheryl Brooks, whose contributions were absolutely fundamental and essential to the production copy preparation, has my special thanks. I am particularly grateful to Eric Valentine, the Quorum Books editor and his copy and production editors for their indispensable advice and guidance through the technical intricacies in preparing the manuscript for production. Finally, I want to thank my wife, Joan, for her sustaining delivery of morning coffee, afternoon tea, and daily understanding, interest, and support for my singular preoccupation, over many months, with writing.

Walter D. Barndt, Jr.

Introduction

We've been a leader and teacher so long that we've forgotten how to be a student.[1]

Michael Mintz
Dow Chemical Corporation

Although the issues involved are complex and subjective and encompass practical differences in point of view, the focus and purpose of this book are simple and straightforward. The intelligence user, not the intelligence provider, must drive the intelligence program. For businesses and most other organized endeavors, information about competitors, what they can and will do, and about the competitive environment is vitally important to their survival and success. It is important because competitors, regulations, laws, economic conditions, technology, social and political movements, industry characteristics, and other factors that are appropriate in the operating environment of a particular enterprise serve to identify opportunities, threats, and limitations to the enterprise's goals, plans, and actions. Thus, reliable, credible, and usable environmental intelligence—competitive intelligence that is consistently and effectively utilized by managers and decision-makers—is a powerful potential source of competitive advantage. Competitive advantage and competitiveness are the objectives of today's global games of business. These are the objectives that motivate managers to plan and act to satisfy organizational and personal agendas.

In the contemporary global environment, where information is readily and often instantly available, access to information is not a differentiating factor. The active and focused gathering, processing, and use of the information are the differentiating factors. The purpose of this book is to introduce new and better ways for intelligence managers, providers, practitioners, or whatever the information product supplier may be called, to provide more effective and usable intelligence to internal customers. Internal customers are those senior managers and key decision-makers within the organization who have significant responsibility for the organization's goals, plans, and actions. The focus for the intelligence initiative is the information user, the information customer. The purpose of any business—and the information supply system is an internal business in any organization—is to get and keep customers. If the internal information supplier satisfies customer needs better than competing suppliers can or will, then the supplier raises the probability of user support and commitment.

At the present time, user support for and commitment to a formal competitive intelligence system are marginal at best or, too often, nonexistent. Information users and decision-makers often have their own informal sources of intelligence that are the conventional and utilized sources. These sources include key advisers, friends, and confidants both within and outside the organization. The information user is more interested in whether the information fits expectations and needs, the credibility of the source (supplier), and the value-added benefit of the information than with the information process. Unfortunately, the competitive intelligence industry and its practitioners have focused on mastering components of the process rather than the value of what the process produces for the user.

The industry, now barely ten years old, is process- and process-technology oriented. It is concerned with how to collect information, sources of information, storage and retrieval systems and quantitatively sophisticated analytical methods and how to package products such as intelligence bulletins, newsletters, and alerts. This undoubtedly has all been of some benefit to the provider in developing an intelligence program. But has or does the program provide significant and sustainable user benefits? In most cases, the answer is no. This is because the intelligence provider has been obsessed with the intelligence process and the products resulting from this process—from the supplier's view rather than from the customer's view. The provider sees the product as useful and usable, and as a technologically sophisticated, differentiated kind of information. The user sees the product as similar to and undifferentiated from conventional information sources and as a decision–making risk factor—both organizationally and personally. What the user wants is information that will reduce or minimize risks, not just more information.[2] The supplier's "business" is in large part defined by the user. Supplier process and technology myopia or myopic definition of the supplier's business will ultimately doom the competitive intelligence provider to continued relative obscurity within the organization.

Myopia is not an unusual condition in a new industry. Producers and suppliers initially see the product, from their perspective, as truly important and useful and just what is needed by the market. The automobile, airline, computer, and banking industries all went through this phase. Some would argue that some of these businesses are still in this phase. Thus, this book is intended to encourage not only practitioners, but all those who serve the industry to shift their thinking toward what the product does for the user rather than what the product is as perceived by the provider. This shift will require looking at the intelligence product from the user's point of view, and understanding what this view is and why the user has this view. In short, it requires an internal intelligence effort to determine what the user wants, needs, and values, and why.

According to John Sedgwick, "A pragmatic school of industrial designers aims to make the controls of a machine—be it a VCR, telephone or nuclear reactor—reflect the people who will use the machine rather than the engineers who want to show off the new technology."[3]

Charles Mauro, an ergonomics consultant, defines complexity as "a fundamental mismatch between the demands of a technology and the capabilities of its user."[4] This by analogy to the corporate intelligence industry today, is the industry's current condition. The intelligence industry has a supply–driven, myopic view that defines the industry in terms of complex and esoteric processes and operations rather than in terms of more useful and direct products that the market—the organization's manager and decision-makers—want, need, understand, value, and will use.[5] A market-oriented intelligence program is difficult to design, develop, and implement. It takes effort, preparation, time, patience, and willingness to risk some independent thinking that may not fit with the organizational culture. This may explain why so few U.S. corporations have made a start toward developing, using, and supporting a formal intelligence program.

This introduction is intended not only to state the rationale and reason for this book, but to summarize its contents, which focus on adding some differentiated value to the demand side of the intelligence process. It is not intended to review or further explore either the need for a formal intelligence program, which is admirably and sufficiently addressed by Jan Herring in the foreword, or the intelligence processes that have been exhaustively addressed in the literature, seminars, and conferences by consultants and others associated with the new competitive intelligence industry. It is time to break some new ground and think of new paradigms or approaches to lift organized and formal intelligence initiatives and efforts off the present no–growth plateau.

THE CONTENTS

This book is organized into two parts around two major themes. Part 1 (Chapters 1–5) looks at missing links in the system. Four parts of the intelligence process thus far have not been adequately considered in intelligence program efforts. The most important missing link is in fact demand side views and perceptions of competitive intelligence. Part 2 (Chapters 6–9) discusses specific ways to add differentiated value to the demand side of the intelligence system. The premise for stating that the intelligence industry is on a no–growth plateau is that there is a bottleneck in the system. There is too much supply and too little demand. In a metaphoric way, this book is intended to suggest ways to clear the blockage by stimulating user demand for the products of a formal competitive intelligence program.

Chapter 1 discusses purpose and the link among intelligence, competitiveness, and competitive advantage. Competitiveness is a popular issue today and as intelligence is a potential source of competitive advantage, it seems appropriate to devote some early discussion to linking the source with a significant and needed purpose. As is true in subsequent chapters, the terminology itself as related to the content—"intelligence" and "competitiveness"—requires some discussion in this chapter. These and other terms mean different things to different people, in different situations and in different organizational settings.

Chapter 2 explores the universe of intelligence. What is the domain and how is this determined? The intelligence domain is likely to have different meanings to different people at different times within the organization. The domain is the intelligence environment that is of most interest and importance to the organization and the user. Here we are also faced with term interpretation issues, such as different meanings of "business" and "competitive intelligence." Chapter 3 addresses the specific issue of terminology.

Chapters 4 and 5 address the issues in understanding, creating, and meeting the demand for the intelligence product. The essential first requirement is to determine what the user needs, wants, and values, and then for the provider to satisfy those needs better than competitors who, in this case, are other intelligence or information risk reduction suppliers. Following this thought process and effectively implementing the required action can result in two kinds of competitive advantage: one for the internal "business," the provider, and one for the organization in the dynamic external competition for markets, product leadership, and resources.

A model of the first section of this book might look like this:

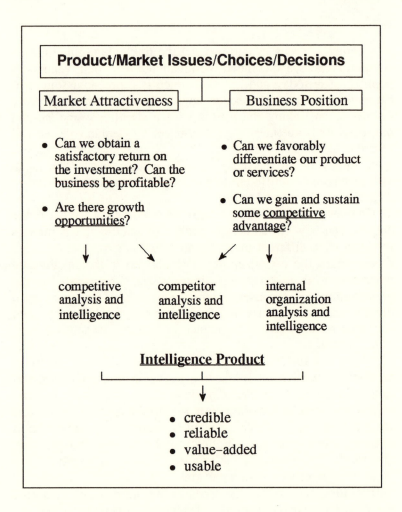

Part 2 (Chapters 6 through 9) concerns value–added issues related to the missing links discussed in Part 1. Chapter 6 considers the question of whether corporate security or counterintelligence programs are part of the intelligence program and system. Protecting the assets, resources, and advantages of an organization is at least as important as assessing a competitor's plans and actions. This leads to a discussion of a vastly underutilized intelligence resource that is critical in competitive assessments and involves profiling

rival decision-makers—the real people who influence or make decisions about competitors' resource allocations, plans, and actions. If personality profiling is an essential part of the intelligence analysis and assessment process and if counterintelligence programs are increasingly a protective necessity, what role should personality profiling play in the security side issue? These questions, issues, and recommendations are addressed by Marshall Heyman in chapters 7 and 8.

The final chapter suggests that the intelligence triad and the linking of business, government, and academe can facilitate the professional development of intelligence providers and the credible further development and acceptance of an intelligence profession.   The model requires the active involvement and participation of the intelligence industry's stakeholders.

The conclusion, Reports from the Battlefield, provides insights concerning the actual and perceived competitive intelligence practices and issues in five companies.

Appendix A provides a summary of research findings based on a survey conducted by the Business Intelligence Study Center in late 1992. The survey was intended to determine what intelligence providers viewed as important characteristics and skills for intelligence providers and what they considered to be the domain of intelligence. Appendix B provides a listing of known research initiatives and proposals intended to further understanding of the purposes, practices, and processes of competitive intelligence systems.

NOTES

1.   In the March 25, 1991 *Fortune* article, "Picking Japan's Research Brains," Mintz also says that American research directors agree that the greatest obstacle to their efforts is the "not invented here" syndrome. This may be a significant problem faced by those who would try to initiate development of a formal intelligence program within their organization. Intelligence was not invented here.

2.   "Many {executives} feel there is an information lack and a significant number identify an 'information glut.'" This quote and

other responses from executives surveyed as summarized in *The Conference Board Report* Number 1027 (1993), "Information for Strategic Decisions," indicate severe inadequacies in their information systems. Respondents cite particular weaknesses in the area of competitive intelligence along with the need for more competitive intelligence that will help them assess and make decisions "on important business matters." The domain of these business matters is generically referred to as information about the future of their industries and customers and obtaining this information "faster than competitors." Thus, there is a recognition that competitive intelligence that is credible, useful, and usable by decision-makers is indeed a powerful source of competitive advantage.

3.   J. Sedgwick, "The Complexity Problem," *The Atlantic Monthly,* March 1993. p. 96

4.   C. Mauro, qtd. in Sedgwick, p. 96

5.   As reported in the *New York Times Magazine* article, "The Future Is Here and It's Ringing," May 16, 1993, many telephone services offered during the past decade have not been enthusiastically received by users. The providers say, "don't worry about that; let the user figure it out."

PART ONE

MISSING LINKS

Chapter 1

Purpose

Competitive: pertaining to, involving or decided by competition. (Competition: the act of competing. Rivalry between two or more persons or groups for an object desired in common usually resulting in a victor and a loser but not necessarily involving the destruction of the latter.) Well-suited for competition, having a feature that makes for successful competition.[1]

"Competitive" and "competition" have standard definitions that give us a basis for the use, meaning and perhaps, substance of these terms in communication and discussion with others. Presumably, a competitor is a person, group, or organization that is actively and directly involved in the rivalry or competition. Relatively, competitor may or may not be competitive. That is, competitors can be characterized as exhibiting some level or degree of competitiveness. However, "competitive*ness*" is not as easily defined. The 1993 New York Mets baseball team was in competition with its National League competitors, but whether they were competitive or not, their degree of competitiveness is debatable. The Mets' competitiveness more often resulted in losing than in winning games. I am not exactly sure how to define "competitiveness," but it must have something to do with individual and organizational resources that are available, and how these resources are used as determinants of a relative competitive position. "Competitiveness" is not easily defined. The purpose of this chapter is not to define competitiveness, but to suggest that the primary purpose for a formal competitive intelligence program is to improve an organization's competitive position.

Strangely enough, "competitiveness" which seems to be derived from a defined word, does not appear to be a word; at least a word found in a standard dictionary. This is very odd, as "competitiveness" is a commonly used term: "Competitiveness is a big word in D.C.,"[2] the President's Council on Competitiveness, and so on. "Competitiveness" is a current buzzword. It is related to the anxieties and efforts of U.S. corporations to improve their competitive positions. Ralph Nader erroneously describes competitiveness as "a strategy by global corporations to reduce our rights and standard of living to the standard of the Koreans."[3] Robert Reich, the current Secretary of Labor, is reportedly fond of saying that "Rarely has a term ["competitiveness"] in public discourse gone so directly from obscurity to meaninglessness without an intervening period of coherence."[4] Some see the term as related to a national industrial, technological, or economic policy. The 1992 Delta Airlines leasing agreement with Airbus Industrie was seen, not surprisingly, by Boeing, as a blow to competitiveness. The concept of competitiveness at Boeing as reported by *Business Week*, means "Managing for World–Class Competitiveness," and is being implemented in a four–day course for all Boeing managers and employees.[5] It is intended to encourage innovation and efficiency in every area.

"Competitiveness" may be general or specific, objective or subjective. Why bother with it as a chapter topic when there are other more widely used terms to link competitive intelligence to a purpose such as "planning," "strategy," or "winning"? In so many ways the term reflects, in various shades and meanings, the entire scope, interest, and effort of American corporations today—to make money, to grow, and to survive.[6] Or, as the International Management Development Institute (IMD) 1992 World Competitiveness Report characterizes it: "Competitiveness is . . . a common term used to refer to an economic effort that first seeks survival and then prosperity for a person, an organization or a national economy."[7]

The IMD document explanation of "competitiveness," is a relatively useful one. Implicit in being competitive is the will to risk an investment of resources. Implicit also is a hierarchy of needs and some goals that have both personal and institutional application. Also implied, as a matter of seeking to be or becoming competitive, are many, if not all, of the usual managerial requirements or imperatives found in any organizational setting. These requirements include plans, actions, decisions, implementation, processes and products, personal and organizational values, profitability and growth, trade-offs and risks. Competitiveness is really an umbrella term for all the latest thinking that is associated with the term: total quality, customer satisfaction and service, employee empowerment, flexibility and adaptability, globalization, restructuring and performance measures such as market share and costs.

"Competitiveness" is, most important, a relative term. It concerns our performance relative to the performance of something else—a standard as in benchmarking, or a comparison with competitors' performance. In short, "competitiveness" is a measure of personal and organizational effort to gain an edge, an advantage, to achieve something. It is a term, as are others in the corporate vocabulary, that defies a uniformly acceptable definition. It may be intellectually stimulating and perhaps even useful to propose a definition and to debate and argue the relative merits of the possibilities. In the context of this book it would be neither particularly stimulating nor useful. "Competitiveness" has to do with an edge, an advantage, and that is why it is a useful term. It is the *most* useful term for competitive intelligence providers to link with their intelligence efforts, interests, and programs. An edge is what really concerns and interests managers. This is *not* the link today between intelligence and purpose. This is a mistake, and one reason why there is a demand side/user bottleneck.

The stated and conventional purposes of formal competitive intelligence programs are to provide information about the appropriate organizational environment, to identify threats and opportunities, to avoid (unpleasant) surprises, to improve planning, to raise the probability of "good" decisions being made, to reduce both organizational and personal risks, or at least to better evaluate risk/reward options and forecasts. In thinking about these usual, conventional, and repetitive purposes, one can conclude that this is the result of learned, text–driven, and conventional thinking. Defining the purpose of intelligence in these conventional ways is what organizational managers have been doing or trying to do for a very long time.[8]   It is nothing new or different.   "Competitive intelligence" can then be viewed by managers as just another term for old and conventional corporate processes and procedures. This is an important cause of and reason for the rather negative or disinterested view of formal competitive intelligence by corporate CEOs. It is easily related to top management's lack of long–term, enthusiastic support and commitment to a new initiative such as a formal intelligence program.   In short, trying to link the new competitive intelligence resource to the old, powerful ways of thinking, planning, acting, and deciding is the trap of conventional wisdom. As William Pfaff says, "The practical function of con–ventional wisdom is to save people from original thought. It makes life easier for everyone even though the eventual costs may be large."[9]   The trap in this case resides in trying to link the new resource of competitive intelligence with conventional processes that are tied to conventional purposes and with often unsatisfactory results.

Clearly, formal intelligence programs—indeed, any initiative requiring resources and support—must be linked to some purpose. That purpose must be viewed as useful and necessary by the program users and supporters. Further, the initiative product must be viewed as being credible, having value, and having actionable properties. While these product attributes are discussed in subsequent chapters, the intent of this first chapter is to set the stage for the scenes that will follow. The initial step is to link the intelligence effort with some different, but related and more positive, real purpose that is viewed as singular, continuous, and of vital importance and high–priority interest to the CEO. Competitiveness, an edge or an advantage, is the priority. Competitiveness is the wanted and needed product of all organized activity. Intelligence is part of this activity.

All the rest, all the conventional purposes of intelligence, are simply the usual bits and pieces that are available from a variety of known and well–established competitive sources. These traditional sources include market researchers, financial analysts, patent lawyers, and others who provide management with information. For formal competitive intelligence programs to be successful and to prosper, they must be disassociated (not physically, but conceptually) and differentiated from these usual information sources. The place to initiate this differentiation is with a real purpose. Competitiveness is the purpose. It is the "sizzle" that will sell the steak–or perhaps today, the stir fry.

What is called for are two bold new initiatives by those who believe in and want to champion the growth of the new competitive intelligence industry. First is a different way of thinking about the real and essential purpose of competitive intelligence–a paradigm that is different from the "conventional wisdom" paradigm and related to the universal desire for a competitive advantage. Second is to determine what the CEO means by "competitiveness" and "competitive advantage," and to fashion intelligence products to meet the user's competitive advantage perceptions, needs, and expectations.[10] This is the first step in reorienting the intelligence efforts from being provider–driven to becoming user–driven.

This change requires not only a new paradigm or thought process that conceptualizes intelligence. It also requires some fundamental research.[11] The new paradigm requires relating this basic purpose or mission to some user–accepted and user–friendly performance or operational standards of measurement. This implies a capability within a formal intelligence system to provide an assessment of what the information means in terms of a competitive position or advantage that is understood and used by the user. This is why it is essential to determine what competitive position and performance are important and of interest to the user, and what this means in terms of some standard or unit of performance/measurement. The standard or unit of measurement is most likely quantitative. Managers may or may not like numbers, but indeed do depend on them to legitimize and defend their decisions.

However the performance measure is expressed, it must be in terms that the user understands, values, and uses. Intelligence, like management, is not a science, but a real art form. It naturally lends itself to the usual qualitative descriptions of intelligence that negatively characterize its "softness": better decisions, avoidance of surprises, good analysis, and so on. This is not good enough.

Linking competitiveness to intelligence requires finding and developing quantitative measures of performance and results that can be used by users to "measure" the value of the formal intelligence resource. Competitiveness is not soft. It is about resources, resource allocation, advantages, and winning. It can be quantified in terms of investments and returns. The terms may be dollars, yen, percentages, ratios, speed, tolerances, service calls, days, hours, or minutes. Linking competitive intelligence to competitiveness provides a real, positive, and option–laden objective and purpose. Competitiveness as opposed to "avoiding surprises" is a continuous and user–friendly term offering challenge, opportunity, and reward. This term suggests a game, and games have great appeal to managers. The game of competition, of "competitiveness" and the rules of the game, is global.[12] This purpose is both a challenge and an opportunity for intelligence providers.

The meaning and purpose of information and intelligence should drive the process, as opposed to the reverse situation common today, in which the process drives the purpose. The intelligence user must see the purpose and the products of the intelligence process to be of top–priority interest and importance. This then helps define an effective process for and the domain and scope of an intelligence program.

NOTES

1. Random House, *Dictionary of the English Language*, 2d ed., 1987.

2. The *Wall Street Journal*, July 1, 1992. By the end of June 1992, 547 competitiveness bills had been introduced in Congress. The proposals in these bills range from tax changes, banning imports and changing antitrust laws, to corporate bailouts and a host of other initiatives. There may not be 547 meanings or definitions attached to the word "competitiveness," but there are many and various interpretations, and they are not linked in any coherent way to the idea of a "competitiveness" policy.

3. Ibid.

4. Ibid.

5. *Business Week*, March 1, 1993.

6. R. A. Pitts and G. C. Snow, *Strategies for Competitive Success* (New York: Wiley, 1986, p. 9). The authors relate competitive advantage (as an expression of competitiveness) to a measure of profitability, specifically "any feature of a business firm that enables it to earn a high return on investment despite counter pressure from competitors."

7. It is suggested that a competitiveness effort is a strategic or political choice. The report further suggests that these efforts will be technology, market, and process driven. These efforts will be more or less successful depending on collective and individual values, plan implementation, appropriate resources (economic and human), and abilities to facilitate and manage change.

8. This idea is addressed in *The Conference Board Report* Number 1021, February 1993, "Challenging Conventional Thinking for Competitive Advantage." The challenges are related to: (1) discontinuity-redefining business; (2) breaking down internal and external boundaries; (3) displacing conventional beliefs about products and services; and (4) vision and fostering creativity.

9. William Pfaff, "Perils of Policy," *Harpers*, May 1987, p.72.

10. A senior executive at a major computer company says that "competitive advantage is achieved when a business looks at the market in a different way than its competitors." The challenge for the intelligence provider here is to determine what the executive means by "different."

11. Some useful information linking competitive intelligence to (bottom-line) performance may emerge from a current study being conducted by B. Jawarski and L. Chee Wee as reported in the *Competitive Intelligence Review*, vol. 3, Nos. 3/4, Fall 1992/Winter 1993 and to members attending the 1993 annual Society of Competitive Intelligence Professionals conference. The researchers suggest, at present, only an indirect link between competitive intelligence and performance that has to do with: (1) more positive relationships among the internal functional areas of the firm; (2) higher-quality strategic plans; and (3) increases in the Strategic Business Unit's knowledge of the market/business environment. Conceptually, they argue that these three factors serve to increase business performance. Further definition of "more positive,"

"higher-quality," and specific "knowledge" would be helpful and perhaps will be included in the final report.

12. Paul Kennedy in his book, *Preparing for the Twenty-First Century*, p. 54, quotes Robert Reich, the Secretary of Labor: "The very idea of an American economy is becoming meaningless, as are the notions of an American corporation, American capital, American products and American technology." Reich in the introduction to his book, *The Work of Nations*, New York: Alfred A Knopf, 1991, p.3, says that "There will no longer be national economies . . . . "

REFERENCES

Barndt, W. D., Jr. "Linking Competitor Intelligence to Competitiveness. "*Competitive Intelligence Review*, vol. 3, no. 2, Summer 1992, 26–30.

Jacobsen, R. "The 'Austrian' School of Strategy." *Academy of Management Review*, vol. 17, no. 4, 1992, 782–807.

Kennedy, P.1992 *Preparing for the Twenty-First Century*. New York: Random House.

The World Competitiveness Report. International Management Development Institute, Lausanne, Switzerland, 12th ed.,1992.

Chapter 2

Scope and Domain

Because not only government but many other types of organizations operate in an environment characterized by a competitive struggle with adversaries, the concept of intelligence might be applied to them as well . . . some researchers try to extend the concept to business corporations. . . . I do not consider these possible extensions of the term intelligence.[1]

A. N. Shulsky does not tell us why he does not consider extending the concept of intelligence to business, but he may well be right in limiting it to the national security concerns of governments. If intelligence is generally considered to be information that is processed and organized to meet the policy, planning, and decision needs of top management, then the scope and domain of government intelligence may not be entirely or, in many cases, even remotely applicable to a corporate intelligence system. This is because of at least three critical reasons. First, the wide-ranging activities that are within the scope of national security intelligence programs—covert operations, espionage, double-agents, technical collection methods, and encription—are legally and generally stated by business managers as ethically and esoterically inappropriate and unnecessary in the private sector. Although the intelligence system or generic intelligence process for government and business may be much the same as indicated in Figure 2.1, the essential elements and activities are different. The figure has been adapted from *Intelligence: The Acme of Skill*, published by Public Affairs, Central Intelligence Agency. Second, the national security model is intended to guide and support presidential policy and decision–making. Corporate information systems including competitive intelligence programs, are intended to provide guidance and support at all levels of planning and decisions—from top–level strategic to lower–level tactical and operational.

Finally, and most important, intelligence does not necessarily have the same meaning to business managers as it does for senior government officials and presidents. Business managers may use data, information, rumor, gossip, knowledge, intuition, and experience in various mixes that can characterize the intelligence that is needed to make decisions.

Figure 2.1

The Intelligence System/Process

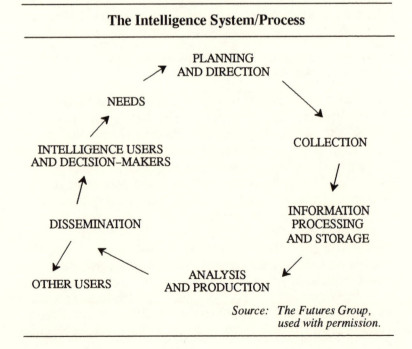

Source: *The Futures Group,
used with permission.*

The meaning and interpretation of discrete system factors is a learned and internalized intelligence process used by the intelligence provider and is not yet a formal, institutionalized intelligence process. The resultant "intelligence," or implications or conclusions derived from the intelligence system are the result of a personalized system and thought process. The scope and domain of corporate intelligence (what information is to be collected and processed and the parameters or boundaries for information gathering) and the sources and types of information to be systematically processed are in reality defined by the intelligence user. The intelligence scope and domain are defined by what the user thinks is needed for the planning or decision-making situation, and the user's perception of the planning or decision universe. "Intelligence" and its scope is what the user thinks it is and how it is intended to be used. While this approach and process can be characterized and portrayed, it is at present not clearly understood by the intelligence provider. Figure 2.2 suggests another way to view the uncertain dimensions of the intelligence scope and domain.

Figure 2.2

Intelligence Scope and Domain	
SCOPE	**DOMAIN**
	Strategic/Tactical/Operational/Personal
• data	information to be collected and its
• information	sources must be specifically related
• rumor	to what the user wants, needs, and
• gossip	expects in terms of the level and type
• knowledge	of decision to be made.
• experience	
• evaluation	

INTELLIGENCE SCOPE AND DOMAIN

While the competitive intelligence industry—consultants, internal academics, providers, and the Society of Competitive Intelligence Professionals (SCIP)—uniformly propose that what is needed by users (and thus the scope) is processed, assessed, and analyzed information, the reality of the managerial planning and decision-making process is often contrary to this model of intelligence.

Figure 2.3

Intelligence Stakeholders' Different Perceptions of Scope and Domain		
	Scope	**Domain**
Consultants	• Broad	• Strategic • High Level
Academics	• Broad	• Strategic • High Level
SCIP	• Broad	• Strategic • High Level
Providers	• Uncertain	• Uncertain

Users	• Narrow to Broad
	  But:
	• Specific Information
		• Specific interests
		  and priorities
		• Specific Decisions

As characterized in Figure 2.3, the dichotomy between what the industry is advising and what users are doing poses enormous resource investment uncertainties for the program. The provider's dilemma is in determining the appropriate scope and domain. The appropriate scope and domain are defined by the user. There are many examples of the scope and domain definition problem that individually and collectively result in less than successful and effective corporate formal intelligence efforts, processes, and products for both the user and the provider.

The Business Intelligence System is one of only a few books that may be helpful to the intelligence provider in terms of understanding and formulating a corporate intelligence system.[2] The authors discuss organizational needs and resource limitations as factors in defining the scope and domain of "business intelligence" activity. They are indeed factors, but the most important factor is the user. They further suggest that domain encompasses the following possible areas: current competitors; economic environment; potential competition; social and community environment; growth opportunities; demographics; technical environment; supplier; markets; acquisition candidates; and the political and regulatory environment.

Discussion of domain does little to help the intelligence provider determine the appropriate key domain areas in which to focus investment and effort. This is because intelligence—and thus the scope and domain of intelligence—is defined and set by the user. The information to be collected and the information sources should be related to the user's needs, wants, and purposes for intelligence.

One major chemical company has simply adapted the above list of eleven factors as its intelligence domain, and the intelligence staff has developed a list of sixty-one questions related to these eleven generic areas.[3]   This has become the basis for this organization's intelligence program. It is provider process–driven, not user process– and system–driven. While the adopted domain model has had some application to a one–time intelligence project requirement, it is woefully incapable of responding to the day–to–day and other less lofty, but equally important competitive or competitor information needs of its users. This has resulted in a lack of direction and focus on the part of the intelligence staff in responding to the real needs, processes, and systems of the users, and in a recent 50 percent reduction in the intelligence staff. One further example will serve to illustrate the problems that exist for providers in not clearly defining and agreeing on the scope and domain of the intelligence system with the users. This example, as contrasted with the "global" domain, suggests the perils of a very limited and functionally related definition of scope and domain.

A major university school of management recently offered a

three-day competitive intelligence seminar for marketing and market research managers. The targeted participants were defined by the seminar content: marketing plans, product development, and market research. This was the defined universe of intelligence for strategies and counterstrategies. This may have been a useful and informative market or market research intelligence seminar, but unfortunately, it also suggests that this is the domain of competitive intelligence. This is not very helpful guidance for the intelligence provider. Market and marketing decisions are only part of inter-related business decisions concerning the risks and payoffs associated with product/market choices. While eleven areas may be too broad, they do have the merit of suggesting the interrelated and complex nature of resolving investment and resource allocation questions and the associated decision risks for both the organization and the decision-maker. Further, this narrow seminar view of the scope and domain of competitive intelligence is, again, process- and provider-driven rather than user-driven.

It is interesting to observe that the overwhelming majority of responses to Question 2 of the survey, which is presented and discussed in Appendix A, fell into one of two categories. Either the intelligence providers, who were the respondents, described the domain of intelligence as encompassing the global model or stated that they either did not understand the question or did not know. Only three responses suggested that the domain should be user-driven (i.e., "the domain is whatever the user says it is").

Perhaps more specifically, the scope and domain are defined by the user's needs and purposes for "intelligence. " It can be argued that the user may not be able (or willing) to articulate or define the need or purpose, and therefore the intelligence provider must opt for the functional, generic, or macro domain approach. This argument is unnecessary and indeed irrelevant if the provider understands that the basic and specific scope and domain are associated with the user's agenda. There is a "core" domain that the user identifies and that can then be shaped or expanded as appropriate by a skilled and experienced provider.

If the scope and domain of intelligence pose a problem and uncertainty for the provider and result in a frustrating, less than effective, and too often short-lived competitive intelligence program, what can be done to give more useful, specific, and focused guidance to intelligence providers? What can be done to gain the long-term commitment and support of the CEO for a formal intelligence program? The solution, the answer, is quite simple to state and understand. Make the program user-driven. Position it as having credibility, value, and application for the user, and not supply- or supplier-driven.

To do this requires determining what the user wants, needs, and values. Provider initiatives for determining these basic user requirements for information are discussed in the following three chapters, which are concerned with additional missing links in the system. Scope and domain are what the user thinks and says they are, and may or may not bear any relationship to what the industry experts and practitioners say they are. Chapters 1, 2, and 3 serve as an introduction to the major focus of this book—that a new, user-driven intelligence program initiative is needed if the supply-driven intelligence blockages are to be relieved.

Before proceeding to Chapter 3 and the important issue of terminology, we should consider another view of domain as an internal organizational issue. Competitive intelligence systems, functions, and positions overlap and compete with other more established organizational information or intelligence sources. These more traditional sources include a wide range of functional activities that are in place to scan and report on the various environments that are appropriate to the organization's business. These activities include market and customer research and information collection and assessment of technological, political, economic, demographic, social, labor, and competitor actions, changes, and trends. In most organizations, these activities and their domain are conventionally defined by the department, group, or function responsible for the activity. Marketing, R&D, legal, personnel, the library, and planning all have their turf, their domain, well-established and recognized relative to this newer activity of competitive intelligence. The internal domain or territory of competitive intelligence is murky at best. This murkiness or uncertainty is related to two organizational issues concerning competitive intelligence.

First, there is the question of what competitive intelligence is and is supposed to do that is different from the other information activities existing within the organization. Is CI a new and value–added information system that complements but is different from other information systems? Is CI a new "packaging" term for traditional management information systems or strategic information systems? Or is CI an attempt to integrate and co-ordinate the processes and products of the existing organizational information systems?

The second question concerns personnel responsibilities that could be considered as defining the internal domain of competitive intelligence. Is the librarian part of the CI system or of the library (or information specialist) system? Where does the salesperson, engineer, scientist, planner, or economic analyst fit or belong?

The point is that the internal domain of CI has yet to be defined. Within the organization, it is often in some temporary shelter rather than a home. This position is so unclear that it is viewed as suspect and threatening by those in the established information systems. It has no unique or differentiating identity—and identity is important. This is one reason the library (or information specialist) members within the Society of Competitive Intelligence Professionals have chosen to organize their own SCIP subgroup.

Finally, it is worth noting why basic and fundamental research in the competitive intelligence realm has been whimsical and quite useless in providing a foundation for CI growth and development. How can competitive intelligence be researched when it has yet to be defined in terms of a universe of activity, purpose, and people? The answer is that it cannot, at least not in any useful way that is likely to establish CI demand and acceptance on the part of intelligence users. The scope and domain issue must be resolved before CI can hope to be an established, credible, reliable, and useful activity.

The substantial absence of current useful research concerning the purpose, and domain and scope issues limits our ability to understand and decide how best to favorably position competitive intelligence. This impediment to the development and application of a logical and appropriate CI system can and will be overcome. The need for research on targeted CI issues is increasingly recognized by many providers, consultants, and academics in the industry. However, this should not prevent us from considering that CI is not only a process, discipline, or system, but also a way of thinking about how we compete and make decisions. As Jan Herring has said many times to my CI course students, "competitive intelligence is a management tool for outthinking the competition." Intelligence and its associated processes and systems can also be positioned as a way of thinking about the organization's purpose, goals, and aspirations and the related necessary decisions, plans, and actions. Outthinking the competition means a capability to see our competitive environment differently than our competitors.

NOTES

1. A. N. Shulsky, *Silent Warfare: Understanding the World of Intelligence.* McLean: Brassey's (U.S.), p. 3. I have used this book as a text with mixed results during one recent semester class in a competitive intelligence course. On the one hand, students found the world of government intelligence interesting and informative, and on the other hand, found it difficult, as Shulsky, consistent with the quote at the beginning of this chapter, does not link the content to the corporate world. Nonetheless, this is a book well worth reading by intelligence providers, particularly for the insights into conflicting points of view about intelligence that the reader can readily identify. As an example, the final chapter in Shulsky's book considers the very elusive intelligence issue of domain—what is essential to be collected and analyzed for what purpose.

2. I have also used this book as a text for the intelligence course on several occasions. Chapter 4, "Critical Intelligence Needs," does offer some guidance as to the kinds of decisions (i.e., operational and strategic) that serve to define the intelligence that managers need, but does not address the related questions regarding the why, when, and how of managerial decision-making that the intelligence provider must understand. Other chapters offer useful insights into intelligence processes and organization. "Competitive advantage" (in the title) is not defined.

3. This information was provided by my research assistant, G. Sparzo, in a 1992 internal memorandum based on extensive company intelligence organization and system research. The memorandum

was intended to provide the basis for a possible case study.

REFERENCES

Gilad, B. and T, 1988. *The Business Intelligence System: A New Tool for Competitive Advantage.* New York: AMACOM.
Shulsky, A. N. 1991. *Silent Warfare: Understanding the World of Intelligence.* McLean: Brassey's (U.S.).

Chapter 3

Terminology

Unless we can agree on the meaning of a word in the context of a discussion, it is difficult to find much value in a discussion that centers on the word. When I talk about "strategy" in my classes I often cite examples and practices that give specific meaning to the term and may have some learning value for the students. Thus there may be value in the discussion, but the value has nothing to do with the word "strategy."[1] The word "strategy" is irrelevant to the discussion because, as it has too many meanings in itself, the word has no meaning. This is because strategy is used so frequently, with so many variations, and often so mindlessly that a specific, common, and agreed–upon meaning by the user and the provider, in spite of dictionary definitions, is quite impossible. We have organizational strategy, business strategy, market strategy, investment strategy, and competitive strategy. There are also strategy derivations as in strategic planning, thinking, management, choices, and moves, and quite possibly even strategic strategies.[2]

One of the purposes of a formal intelligence system is to provide the user with information that can be integrated by the user into a strategic planning or decision–making process, whatever that may be. The assumption by the intelligence provider, as strategy is so commonly used in businesses, is that the user is engaged in some vague strategy process or decision and needs some vaguely strategically related information or intelligence. This assumption could be faulty. The user's terminology involved in the particular problem to be addressed or question to be answered may not include the word "strategy" at all. Clues to the user's terminology might be found in phrases such as "what action should be taken," "what's the best decision," "what does this mean," and so on. Even if the word "strategy" is part of the issue, "what are the strategic implications"? The user's meaning of the term may be quite different than the meaning assumed by the provider. The word "strategy", although a convenient word, should be banned by businesses.[3] It is too often meaningless, redundant, and lacking in specificity. It may be appropriate for military or government organizations where the organizational meaning is specific, accepted, and understood, but in business its value is questionable. However, the discussion in this chapter is not about strategy in any of its forms. It is about the common problem of differences in terminology between providers and users.

The point is that unless the user uses the terminology and agrees with the provider on the meaning of the terminology, it is unproductive to use the terminology in designing intelligence efforts, communications, and products. A related obvious point is that among the user's needs, wants, and values to be clearly understood by the provider are words and terms used by and important to the user. This leads us to examine the principal terminology in our ill–defined domain—intelligence, business intelligence, competitive intelligence, and competitor intelligence.

Three somewhat conflicting definitions of intelligence illustrate the point of confused terminology.

The Central Intelligence Agency

"Knowledge and foreknowledge of the world around us"—the prelude to presidential decisions and actions.[4]

A Consultant's Definition of Intelligence

Intelligence = actionable and organized information,[5] that is, processed information (credibility, reliability, and usability)—the process; and presentation of the intelligence to intelligence users in a style, format, and time that will encourage acceptance and use of the intelligence—the product.[6]

An Intelligence Professional's Definition of Intelligence

In the book *Honorable Treachery*,[7] the author states that "Intelligence is information. Specifically, it is information about an adversary that is useful in dealing with him". This definition comes closest to a meaning that would be a useful starting point for both intelligence providers and users, at least in the context of concerns about competitors.

Are these definitions useful or appropriate in the business context? Do managers and decision-makers in business consciously think of or use/articulate the word "intelligence" when they consider whatever they regard as relevant and important to know in making decisions? Is "intelligence" part of the user's working vocabulary? Is it "information" or "data" or something else that the user uses? Again, the point is that providers of "intelligence" must know if "intelligence" is part of the user's vocabulary and if not, why not? The provider should choose a word for the intelligence product that is user-friendly—that is "actionable" by the user and used by the user.

Why might "intelligence" be an inappropriate term? Possibly because of:

- Association with national intelligence work—covert, spying, espionage. A negative connotation.

- Association with war and a wartime environment. To win, to defeat the enemy. Unless business managers actually consider that they are at war (with their competitors or stakeholders), it is unlikely that "intelligence" will have the same positive, credible association that it does in the military forces. Although books, articles and quotations relating business to warfare are popular today, there is no proof that U.S. business managers believe that they are a military force at war. In warfare, it is usually advisable to fight one enemy on one front. In business, there are often numerous enemies (competitors, regulators, unions, etc.) on numerous fronts. Thus, while principles of warfare may be fun to read, they are difficult and perhaps impractical in any extended way, to incorporate into business planning and operations.

Does business really need the word "intelligence" in its terminology, or would "information" or "knowledge" be more concise, understood and actionable? One could reasonably answer yes to intelligence if the word has some positive, specific meaning within the organization and for the intelligence user. In any event, as words can often be misunderstood or misinterpreted and thus the purpose of the function or action that is associated with the word can be obscured, minimalized, or ignored, terminology can be worth considering. Terminology could be just one of many possible obstacles to support for and acceptance of a formal intelligence program. Among other possible demand side impediments would be the use of the word "intelligence" in providing those in the intelligence program with a sense of importance and comfort that is not enthusiastically shared by others in the organization. With these caveats in mind, I will use "intelligence" in this book to mean the product derived from the information-gathering process and offer a definition of this and other key terms that will be used throughout the chapters and their discussion topics.

1. *Intelligence.* Information that is analyzed, assessed, or other-wise appropriately processed by either intelligence providers or users and that is used by managers and decision-makers for planning, action, and decision purposes with the objective of gaining or sustaining a competitive advantage.

2. *Competitive Intelligence.* Information that is concerned with events and actions external or internal to the organization that will affect organizational plans, actions, and decisions. This is close to the commonly used term "business intelligence," but is preferred for two reasons. "Competitive" is a more focused word and suggests a link with competitiveness and competitive advantage. "Business" is less focused and suggests to the manager or decision-maker a broad set of possibly conflicting and competing information and sources. Second, "business," intelligence as the term is commonly used today,

fails to include internal information concerning option strategy, resource availability, and operational capabilities. That information is essential in planning, actions, and decisions.

3. *Competitor Intelligence.* Information that is concerned with present and potential market and resource competitors, and what they can and will do. This is a specific sub–element of competitive intelligence that is always a factor in any organization's plans, actions, and decisions. Economic, political, or technological intelligence may also be factors.

4. *Intelligence User.* Any person in the organization for whom information, however processed, is appropriate, needed or wanted. To avoid multiple words and to simplify the reader's tasks, I will at times use the term "CEO" in place of "user." As the formal intelligence function is primarily designed to serve the organization's key decision–makers, I will also use this term interchangeably with "senior manager" or "top management."

5. *Intelligence Provider.* Any person in a formal intelligence program involved with the competitive intelligence process, products, or management of the program. It is recognized that different persons may have different responsibilities for intelligence—collectors, analysts, researchers, planners, information specialists, and so on—but often, one person either does all of the process and product tasks or oversees the work done by others who are peripheral to the function. To sort all of this out now would be extraordinarily difficult, and would only serve to confuse the reader and to obscure the essential purpose of this book. This essential purpose is to discuss and suggest ways to clear the intelligence demand side bottleneck by focusing, after ten years of industry attention to the supply side, on the user or demand side. The user is the key to clearing the bottleneck, to stimulating demand, and ultimately to providing the support for and commitment to a formal intelligence program.

Offering definitions in an industry whose purpose and domain are yet to be adequately defined is both risky and, probably, provocative. However, terminology is a real and legitimate issue in communication and one of the useful starting points in stimulating demand for formal competitive intelligence programs.

NOTES

1. *Strategy*: "A plan, method or series of maneuvers or strategems *(strategem*: a plan, scheme or tricks for surprising or deceiving an enemy) for obtaining a specific goal or result." This definition from the *Random House Dictionary of the English Language,* 2d ed., 1987, and its related definition of the unfortunate word "strategize" ("to make up or determine a strategy"), illustrate the mindless and generic usage associated with this word. Strategy is part of our real language, but one does wonder why.

2. Mickey Kantor, the U.S. Trade Representative, used this phrase ("strategic strategies") while talking about trade with Japan on the MacNeil-Lehrer news hour, April 25, 1993. Could terminology be part of our larger problems?

3. "He (William L. Langer) was told. . . . never to use the word strategy in his communications, for this would antagonize the armed services" This quote from Robin W. Winks' scholarly and illuminating book, *Cloak & Gown: Scholars in the Secret War, 1934-1961* (New York: Morrow, 1987), 75, provides an example of the possible embarrassments that can be associated or derived from terminology that is, often quite innocently, ill-chosen. Winks does not explain why the word "strategy" coming from Langer's Research and Analysis branch of the Office of Strategic Services during the early years of World War II should antagonize the military. However, one might guess that "strategy" was the military services' turf and responsibility and therefore its use by the scholars in the Research and Analysis branch who had no appreciation or knowledge of strategy, would render their reports quite useless and unreliable.

4. This definition is taken from *"Intelligence: The Acme of Skill,"* The Central Intelligence Agency, Public Affairs Office.

5. This is the core meaning and requirement of intelligence as suggested by many consultants and practitioners in the industry. That intelligence must be "actionable" was first suggested as an essential requirement to be met in an intelligence program by Jan

Herring at a 1989 intelligence workshop in St. Louis.

6. Gil Press of Digital Equipment Corporation is close to this definition of competitive intelligence when he states (in a presentation at the 1993 SCIP annual conference) that business intelligence "is the process of transforming data . . . . into information . . . . and of transforming information into analysis." He characterizes analysis as "understanding its meaning and implications (in light of the organization's specific objectives, strengths and weaknesses, culture, experience, organizational structure, business processes, etc.)." The implication is that internal analysis (intelligence) is part of the process. In any event, much or all of the transforming may be redundant if the intelligence user's view of intelligence is data or information or rumor or some other form of information that is converted by the user to "intelligence."

7. *Honorable Treachery*, by G. J. A. O'Toole (Atlantic, 1991). O'Toole was employed by the CIA, and this definition of intelligence appears on page 1 of his long, informative, and well-documented book.

Chapter 4

The System and the Intelligence User

A formal intelligence program which is not initiated, or at least strongly backed *and used* by top management is doomed to obscurity and lack of real influence on decisions.[1]

The key to clearing the intelligence bottleneck of oversupply and too little demand is to create the conditions in which the intelligence program user wants the intelligence program product. The intelligence program provider or manager has this responsibility. If the user wants the product, the intelligence program is in a far better position to be utilized and supported by the user. Again, the term "user" will be synonymous with CEO, top management, or senior management. Although it can be argued that intelligence users can be anyone in the organization, the assumption is that a formal intelligence program is (to be) designed to meet the intelligence needs of the organization's senior officers who are responsible for any important organizational decisions, plans, and actions. It can also be argued that if top management initiates a formal intelligence program, the user and support issues would not be issues, or at least the same issues. However, the great majority of such program initiatives during the past several years have originated at a middle or lower level of management by someone who sees the value of an intelligence program and has taken steps to develop a program. In any case, this chapter provides information and suggestions to help the intelligence provider stimulate demand. It all begins with the user. In the intelligence system, users and their "business" are one of the missing links in the system.

A formal intelligence program, as contrasted to an informal program, would have some organizational resource support (office space, personnel, or budget), some stated organizational focus or purpose and prescribed operational guidelines. Somewhere in the organization some manager would have to approve a proposed formal program and allocate some resources to launch and sustain the program. This might be done at the business unit or division or department level. Top management at the corporate level may not strongly back or use the program service. It is also unusual in large companies for the CEO or top management to *initiate* a formal intelligence program. Among the handful of companies often cited as having such a program—Kodak, AT&T, McDonnell Douglas, Corning, Southwestern Bell, Digital Equipment and Motorola,[2] —only Motorola is known to have established a formal system at the initiative of the CEO.[3] While it may indeed be desirable for top management to initiate and have a strong *commitment* to a formal program, most initiatives do not originate at the top. Lower-level initiatives are not necessarily doomed to obscurity or lack of influence. The conventional wisdom that top management must initiate a program as a prerequisite for success is suspect and should not be a deterrent to developing an effective program. The intelligence user can be brought into and can buy into the system whatever its origin. To be successful, a (formal intelligence) program must meet a need and provide some value-added benefit to program users, be effectively implemented, and be credible. The needs, benefits, and credibility issues from the intelligence user's perspective will be discussed in this chapter.

While intelligence users are, theoretically at least, any managers who control or allocate organizational resources and make decisions affecting organizational resources, plans, operations, and so on, the focus will be on those users who are considered top managers. These users would include the CEO and other senior-level corporate, division, or business unit managers. This is not entirely an arbitrary choice for two reasons. The purpose of a formal intelligence program is to provide senior management with analyzed or processed information—the intelligence product —which will assist these managers in making important strategic and policy decisions. Second, for formal intelligence programs to be successful and to become institutionalized in the long run, support of top managers will be required. Regardless of the initiative source, eventually senior managers must see some value and payoff for the initiative if it is to be institutionalized as a long-term high-priority asset.

Formal (competitive) intelligence is a relatively new concept for business managers. It is only one of many new programs and ideas that compete for the attention and support of top management. For top management, there are enormous personal risks in backing the wrong initiatives. If, for example, the CEO is supposed to provide leadership and support and to champion some change that is synonymous with a new initiative, the CEO is then accountable for: (1) the problems that caused the new initiative to be proposed in the first place; and (2) for the possibility that the initiative will fail. These are risks that the CEO would prefer not to take. If the risk can be minimized by lowering the entry and exit costs for the CEO's commitment to the program, then the probability that the CEO will vigorously support the program is obviously increased. There are two ways to reduce this risk and to gain the enthusiastic support of the CEO. Either the CEO initiates the program (the Motorola model) and thus is committed to it, or some other manager initiates the program (most models) and tries to convince the CEO that the program meets some important needs, provides value-related benefits, and has credibility. For the program initiator/manager to do this requires some clear understanding and "intelligence" about the CEO as an intelligence user. Since this is the most usual model we can examine the user issues from this view.

THE INTELLIGENCE USER/CEO NEEDS
The matrix in figure 4.1 suggests the scope of the user's needs and the range of sources that can meet these needs. This provides a starting point for the intelligence initiator/provider/manager to

build a case for value–added benefits and credibility.

Figure 4.1

**The Intelligence Manager's Model of the
Intelligence User's Needs or Priorities**

Needs/Priorities/Sources

1. Organizational Agenda (OA)
   - growth
   - profitability
   - survival
   - competitiveness
   - quality
   - specific ideas concerning these and other OA needs
2. Personal Agenda (PA)
   - short–term
   - long–term
   - risk aversion
   - innovator
   - control
   - loyalty
   - trust
   - involvement
   - personal security
3. Decisions and Process
   - strategic
   - operational
   - technical
   - when
   - how
   - where
   - why
   - qualitative
   - quantitative
4. Organizational Culture
   - maintain/support
   - change

Internal   External   Self

Providers must know which sources the intelligence user draws on (internal to the organization, external to the organization, and self–generated sources such as experiences and intuition or more likely some combination of sources) for information in the user's decision–making and planning process.

ORGANIZATIONAL VALUES

One source of the demand side bottleneck resides in understanding, adapting to, or possibly changing the intelligence user's organizational agenda. What are the "hot buttons," the priority issues, threats, or opportunities that the CEO views as most important for the organization? Unless the intelligence product is related to these hot buttons, the intelligence program will not be viewed as a value–added, credible program. The provider must know what the user needs to deal with these key issues. As suggested in Chapter 1, "competitiveness" is likely to be a current hot topic for the CEO and senior managers. How to survive and prosper in a rapidly changing business environment commands much of senior management's time, attention, and energy. Competitiveness may be thought of in terms of quality, technology, process improvements, government policy, or any number of other specifics or combination of specifics by the user. It is important for the intelligence provider to clearly understand the general and specific institutional concerns of the CEO.

The intelligence product should be shaped to address these concerns. All too often the intelligence provider produces a buffet of information, leaving the bewildered user to somehow select something, rather than a limited intelligence menu that is aligned with the user's needs and priorities. An unintended result may be that the user chooses not to select anything from the intelligence program system. The product buffet is too general and vague to link, from the user's perspective, with some value–added benefits.[4] Competitiveness may or may not be the CEO's key concern. Many CEOs are under enormous pressure from organizational investors and the investment community to provide quick results from organizational initiatives. The initiative may be linked to the latest quick fix theory or idea. It may be "Total Quality Management" and the specific implementation concern may be in "doing it right." Thus, benchmarking competitors or world–class performers may be the specific need.

The point is that if the intelligence provider is going to get the CEO's attention, interest or support, the intelligence products must be closely linked to the CEO's organizational agenda. If the agenda is "quality" then the intelligence analysis and product should be focused on an assessment of the organization's "quality" relative to competitors or best performers and the effects of this assessment on some measure of performance that is important to and used by the CEO. The product must be specifically related to one or a few of the CEO's real organizational concerns, not vaguely presented as strategically important. How can or should the intelligence manager match the product to the user's organizational needs and agenda?

Figure 4.2

The Quality Domain

Quality Factors	Quality Performance Measures	
	Internal	*External*
1. product technology	• costs	• competitors
2. process technology	• customer retention	• world class
3. employee involvement	• project groups	• consultants
4. organization	• idea suggestion	• suppliers
5. suppliers	• processes	• distributors
6. customers	• inventory control	• customers
7. The Baldridge Award	• other	• other

The simple answer is to know your customer, to talk with the user and discuss the user's needs and agenda. But the simple answer requires research, intelligence, and some proactive initiatives by the intelligence provider. If, for example, the priority is quality, what is the quality domain that is important to the CEO?

As suggested in Figure 4.2, the intelligence manager will want to know what specific factors are important to the quality improvement program and, importantly, what measure the user considers important in assessing the organization's relative quality performance. Is the CEO concerned about competitors' quality, world–class quality, supplier relationships, employee motivation and compensation, or other specific factors and sources in the quality domain? Answers to these questions will serve to effectively focus the intelligence process toward producing products that meet the user's organizational agenda.

The remaining problem for the intelligence provider in discussing these issues with the intelligence user(s) is establishing credibility with the user. The user must view the intelligence program, staff, and products as among the reliable, trusted sources of information that are consistently used by the CEO in making decisions and plans and in taking action. The problems and issues of provider credibility will be discussed in Chapter 5.

PERSONAL VALUES

A second set of impediments in the demand side bottleneck is related to the intelligence user's personal agenda concerning what he or she believes or perceives, and how he or she acts or behaves on the job. These personal agenda factors, along with factors of personality, tend to dictate what advice the intelligence user is willing to accept and what influence the intelligence manager is able to exert on the user's decision–making process. In a sense, a personality assessment of the user by the provider is also implicit in understanding agendas and gaining the continuing support and commitment of the CEO for a formal intelligence program. Several examples of possible user values will illustrate the personal agenda impediment issue. Figure 4.3 suggests that there are a number of sources that influence personal agenda characteristics. They can be identified and assessed for use-ful and necessary agenda insights and understanding.

For example, if the CEO has a short attention span, immediate or short–term positive results or a quick fix may be an important factor in planning and action decisions. The user may give lip service support and even intellectually agree with long–term initiatives, but in actual practice will not risk the necessary supportive leadership and actions to implement and develop such an initiative. It is difficult at best to forecast what investments and changes will be needed to assure survival, growth, or profitability by the organization over the longer term. This is especially the case in businesses or industries where rapid changes and increasing complexity in assessing the meaning of political, economic, social and technological changes are becoming more and more the norm. The short–term and day–to–day requirements for actions and decisions by the CEO have the highest priority because they are necessary and are taken with a higher degree of certainty regarding the situation. Thus they are easier to

Figure 4.3

Personal Agenda

The CEO Characteristic

- is risk-averse
- likes a "safe" solution/decision
- other important characteristics

Sources of Characteristic

- personality (see Chapters 7 and 8)
- industry forces influence
- organizational environment
- organization experience
  - previous actions, decisions,
  - performance
- future plans
  - retirement soon
  - promotion
  - protect value of stockholding

---

make and manage.

The CEO may want advice or intelligence that supports what is already believed or known about a given situation. Preconceived ideas and conventional wisdom concerning what is needed or what works or what to do will exert a powerful influence on the user's decisions and actions. Once decisions have been made in this context, it is extraordinarily difficult for the CEO to change this pattern of behavior, particularly if such behavior has in the past been relatively successful. This situation may be analogous to "kill the messenger" (or ignore the message bearing contrary news) syndrome. The provider's analysis may be right or "better," but if it isn't what the CEO believes or wants to hear, the provider's first intelligence briefing may be the last briefing. Independent thought may be desirable, but it will only have value if the CEO values it and the organizational culture supports it. To some degree this situation exists among all senior managers in all organizations. Senior managers become senior managers because they have learned what works, what produces results, and therefore have firm opinions and take actions that are the result of their learned experience. They also have learned what advice and whose advice to accept in formulating these opinions, making decisions, and taking actions. A conventional organizational environment fosters acceptance of conventional wisdom which, if challenged by the intelligence provider, can be risky for the challenger.

Thus, another impediment may be found in the sources of information, advice, or intelligence that the CEO uses, relies on, and trusts in formulating decisions. The user will naturally and more easily accept advice and intelligence from those persons that, through experience, the user knows and trusts. These sources may be among those considered as loyal to the CEO, having recognized expertise or, for whatever reason, those who have more power or influence in the organization than does the user. In any case, source credibility implies a lengthy or close relationship between the user and the sources.[5] The problem for the intelligence provider is that the CEO may not know the person or persons performing the analysis or providing the intelligence. The user and provider may be sufficiently separated by levels of management or space as to make it difficult for the provider to become known as a credible, reliable source of advice and intelligence for the user.[6]

Perhaps in some organizations the CEO may be very concerned about personal security. In the current environment of international unrest, political uncertainty, and acts of terrorism, executive security is a legitimate concern. This may be the central or only formal intelligence interest. Few formal intelligence programs are designed for or capable of addressing this user value.

In any event, the provider must develop insights about the user's personal interests, beliefs, values, and agendas. A personality assessment or some factual indicators of personal characteristics, as discussed in Chapter 8, may be a necessary proactive initiative for the intelligence provider. The CEO's personal agenda will be influenced not only by his or her personality, but by previous organizational experience, perceptions of relevant industry forces and the user's pattern of making decisions. The intelligence product is supposed to help the CEO make better and better informed decisions. For the product to serve this purpose, the intelligence provider must also know in some detail the types of decisions made and the decision processes used by the CEO.

DECISIONS AND PROCESSES

The first question to be answered by the intelligence manager concerns the kinds of decisions that the CEO does or will make. Are they strategic, longer-term, vitally important to the survival of the organization, implying some anticipated future investment or realignment? Are they tactical or short-term decisions? Figure 4.4 is a framework for determining the types of decisions and processes that may be relevant to the intelligence user. Although theoretically strategic planning or thinking is what senior managers do or are supposed to do, it is likely that significantly less time is devoted to these "strategic" type decisions, even if important, than to other types of decisions. In addition to pressure on the CEO for short-term results and performance, it is enormously difficult for the CEO to visualize with some degree of confidence and comfort what will happen and what will be needed in the future. Also in this situation, the intelligence provider has the difficult task of providing the user with credible forecast scenarios, trend evaluations, and future competitive moves and reactions.

Figure 4.4

Decision and Process

Type of Decision	*Decision Process*
• tactical, short-term	• when, under what conditions, how often
• reactive	• where: business office, home, club
• others as appropriate	• why: to solve a problem, postpone a problem resolution
	• fight a fire
	• relies on quantitative/qualitative information
	• seeks advice of others. Who?
	• makes own decisions or "gut" instinct

With the short-term pressures exerted on the CEO and rapidly changing business conditions and environments, it is far more likely that the intelligence user will be more concerned with short-term or operational type decisions, than with strategic decisions. Such tactical decisions, while often reactive and defensive in nature, do, if good decisions, serve to define and set longer-term strategic plans, objectives, and interests. In this case, the user will want current relevant intelligence that will assist the user in determining what to do about a competitor's price reduction, a partner's plan to form a joint venture with a competitor, a product recall, or whether to abandon a product or technology investment.

User decisions may be strategic, tactical, operational, or some combination of a range of decisions. Some decisions may be so sensitive in nature that only a trusted few in the organization will have access to the decision-maker as advisers or intelligence sources. Such closely held decisions would include plant closings, employee reductions, mergers or buy-outs, and other decisions that may adversely affect important organizational stakeholder groups. Such situations pose the greatest difficulty for the intelligence provider and, at the same time, reinforce the absolute requirement for provider credibility with the user.

An example of a situation in which the formal intelligence program manager would probably not have access to the CEO's priority intelligence needs is contained in a 1990 *Wall Street Journal* story concerning American Express. American Express admitted in 1989 that it had engaged in a covert campaign to ruin the reputation of a rival banker, Edmund Safra. Although the then chairman and chief executive officer of American Express, James D. Robinson III, was not directly linked to this operation, senior managers and their advisers were involved in this investigation of a competitor's activities. Even if the intelligence manager was providing information to senior managers about the competitor's organization, it is unlikely, as this was a covert operation, that the provider would have more than partial knowledge of the user's agenda. Senior management's agenda was in fact several agendas, only one of which may have been the stated and "public" agenda. This example also illustrates that often there are games within the game.

In any case, the intelligence provider must understand more clearly the user's decision process and decision agenda if the intelligence program is to provide the user with a credible, value–added, and usable product. Finally, it is important that the provider understand the organizational culture—those sets and patterns of behavior, beliefs, and actions that define the organization and its value system. It is important to know what can be tolerated, what is encouraged or discouraged, and how things work and are done in the organization. These cultural factors also serve to define the CEO's interests, beliefs, and behavior. Provider knowledge of the user's organizational agenda, personal agenda, decision and decision process agenda, the organizational culture, and industry forces and characteristics is essential for a formal intelligence program to have any reasonable chance of successfully competing for organizational resources, recognition, and long–term survival.

What can and should the provider do to better meet the user's needs, add value, and establish credibility? First, know your customer, as a person, as having specific needs, values, and requirements. In part, at least, this gives the provider necessary insight into the customer/user's present and possible future actions, motivations, and agendas.

The intelligence product is a service. It is an intangible product that the user must believe is needed now and at least of equal if not greater value than competing intelligence products. The user is less concerned with the process than the process results. Does the product add value to the user's information processing and decision process now? Is the decision, planning, or action product that results from this process viewed as a better product by the user? Is the intelligence product credible and is the intelligence source reliable?

Knowing the customer allows the provider to tailor the product to the user's agenda, rather than being a product derived from the provider's agenda. Don't try to change the user's agenda unless you are really positioned to do so. Unless you are in the CEO's inner circle of trusted advisers or friends, you will not be in a relatively favorable position to change the user's beliefs, behavior, or actions. Find out who these trusted advisers are that influence that user's decisions. Who does the CEO listen to? Are they other senior officers in the organization, the user's assistant, an industry analyst, an outside consultant, the user's spouse? What are their beliefs and values and what do these sources tell the CEO? Do a brief personality profile of these inner circle members.

Finally, the CEO may know more about the decision issue or situation than you do. Some part of the issue may be hidden. The user may also be an "expert" (or believe himself or herself to be an expert) in some area that is part of the user's agenda. It isn't easy to discover these hidden areas, but it is possible. Study the subject that is in the area of the user's expertise. Listen, talk to people, and attend meetings. Do something that is not in the intelligence provider's job description. Find out what intelligence system the CEO uses. This is the first step in creating intelligence products that are of real value to the user. Providing value-added products for the user will, over time, help provide the intelligence program and manager with credibility.

Again, the main point of this chapter is to know your customer. Regardless of where or why or how a formal intelligence program is (to be) initiated, it cannot succeed or survive unless the customer's needs are met or exceeded. The intelligence provider needs to gather a great deal of intelligence about the user before the provider can develop and deliver a product that the user will value and use. The intelligence product is a factor in the user's decision-making process. The process and resulting decisions pose some degree of risk for the CEO. The CEO would like to reduce the risk. Help the CEO to do so by knowing the sources and the characterstics of the user's agenda.

Two recent (early 1993) surveys illustrate the nature and focus of current intelligence thinking that is supply side-oriented. Participants attending an intelligence conference were asked to respond to seventeen questions, all of which were related to intelligence organization, budgets, and provider activity and which were intended to "enhance the role of competitive intelligence in the organization." None asked the respondent to consider demand side/user questions or issues or what competitive intelligence is desired or requested. The second questionnaire, unrelated to the first, from an intelligence consulting firm asks respondents to answer thirteen questions, again entirely related to supply side processes, activities, and budgets.

Finally, and even though a demand side approach to formal intelligence programs is a preferred approach, it may not be possible in all organizations. Fred Haynes, vice president for planning and analysis at LTV's Missile and Electronic Group, says, "We don't need that kind of person (an intelligence professional or specialist) . . . . The minute you get specialists, the key guys start to forget to think."[7] This situation poses some interesting questions for supply side intelligence and for the intelligence provider as the second key player in the intelligence system link. As James Paige of Xerox says, "There's an awful lot of salesmanship in the corporate intelligence person's job."[8]

NOTES

1. This quote by B. Gilad in his article, 31, "The Role of Organized Competitive Intelligence in Corporate Strategy," strongly implies the value of a demand side, user-oriented approach to formal intelligence program initiatives. The author proposes a strategy for organized intelligence operations that addresses the problems of integrating manufacturing activities with the decision-making process.

2. These companies listed in "Still a Distant Second," *Across the Board* (the Conference Board) November 1991, 47, are also listed in other articles on intelligence. It is not known if SCIP has undertaken an analysis of its membership to identify member organizations represented.

3. Jan P. Herring, who organized and developed the Motorola program in the mid-1980s, suggests that Motorola may be unique in that the initiative for a program came from the then chairman.

4. As the writer of the May 14, 1992 *Wall Street Journal* article, "Quality Programs Show Shoddy Results," 31, states: "Many quality-management plans are simply too amorphous to generate better products and services." The "Baldridge awards may be losing some luster," was the headline in a *Wall Street Journal* article on April 19, 1993. The link between the process and results is not clear.

5. "CEO's Seeking Advice Stay Close to Home," *Wall Street Journal*, August 20, 1991. The article reported that in a survey of ninety CEOs, 62 percent said they consult their senior executives

and 56 percent consult directors in seeking strategic advice. Other sources cited were colleagues in other firms, lawyers, and CPAs.

6. W. M. McGrath, Jr. states in his contribution, "Improving Competitor Intelligence Value to Management," *Advances in Competitive Intelligence* published in 1989 by the Society of Competitive Intelligence Professionals, "two major causes for the underutilization of this powerful resource (formal competitive intelligence): (1) . . . . focus . . . . and data acquisition rather than analysis and decision making; (2) organizationally . . . . competitor intelligence [is] often too far removed from the business decision makers." It is interesting to note that the Society of Competitive Intelligence Professionals replaced "competitor" with "competitive" in its title in 1990.

7. Haynes offers some useful insights into senior management thinking about intelligence in the article, "Federal Sleuthing Experts, Private Intelligence Needs," *Insight*, October 15, 1990, 40.

8. "The New Race for Intelligence." *Fortune*, November 2, 1992, 105. It's salesmanship and more. It's marketing. The intelligence provider is not only a "buyer" of intelligence (know the sources and processes), but a supplier (know your customers).

REFERENCES

Brockhoff, K. "Competitor Technology Intelligence in German Companies". *Industrial Marketing Management*, no. 20, 1991, 91–98.

Gelb, B. D., et al. "Competitive Intelligence: Insights from Executives." *Business Horizons*, January–February 1991, 43–47.

Gilad, B. "The Role of Organized Competitive Intelligence in Corporate Strategy". *Columbia Journal of World Business*, Winter 1989, 29–34.

Harrell, G. D., and M. F. Fors. "Internal Marketing of a Service." *Industrial Marketing Management*, no. 21, 1992, 299–306.

Herring, J. P. "Senior Management Must Champion Business Intelligence Programs." *Journal of Business Strategy*, September–October 1991.

Zajac, E. J., and M. H. Bozerman. "Blind Spots in Industry and Competitor Analysis: Implications of Interfirm (Mis) Perceptions for Strategic Decisions." *Academy of Management Review*, vol. 16. no. 1, 1991, 37–56.

Chapter 5

The System and the Intelligence Provider

The difference between the intelligent and the stupid individual is that the intelligent person can put seemingly unrelated pieces of information together to create a new whole. That's what the corporate intelligence professional does. [1]

As Bernard Reimann suggests, corporate intelligence is the first step toward initiating a successful corporate program. In the same *Fortune* article, J. Prescott of the University of Pittsburgh says: "Unless you address corporate intelligence, you're not going to get off square one in dealing with global competitiveness." [2] The implication in both statements is that corporate (competitive) intelligence professionals, being intelligent persons, spend a great deal of time gathering and putting together unrelated and possibly irrelevant information about something and thus create something less than a "new whole." One further implication is that the corporate intelligence bottleneck problem lies not with the intelligence provider who is addressing corporate intelligence and putting information together, but with someone else. Who is this someone else? Of course, senior management or key intelligence users who don't understand, appreciate, and support the corporate intelligence program and the program's intelligence staff. While this may be true, the intelligence problem is not with the user. It is a problem caused and generated by years of neglecting to systematically understand the demand side of the intelligence system, the users and their needs and agendas.

As has been suggested in previous chapters, the real first step in developing and sustaining an effective and successful formal intelligence program is to convince the user that the program will and does provide credible, valuable, and usable information. The realm of corporate intelligence has been exhaustively addressed for the past ten years in books, articles, seminars, meetings, and consultant workshops. Unfortunately, the realm has been mainly concerned with the supply side process and technology and the net result is very little gain for a great deal of effort. Formal competitive intelligence programs are at best on hold in corporate America. Within the supply side realm, intelligence provider issues have been addressed on the basis of a faulty assumption. The assumption is that if the gathering, analyses, and technology of the intelligence process are brilliant enough, the program will be a success. This is a faulty assumption. The provider rarely has a view of the whole system, works usually with only a piece of the system, and often is only part-time. The Society of Competitive Intelligence Professionals, in a 1989 survey,[3] indicates that competitive intelligence workers spend half their time on planning and data collection and less than one-third on analysis. The intelligence provider is often someone in the library or marketing or engineering who collects information that may or may not be evaluated, and who, in any event, is very unlikely to be able to know or to find all the "unrelated pieces" in order to create a "whole" picture. In fact, it may be inappropriate for the intelligence provider to present the user with processed information that points to some course of action. The user may prefer to provide the pointers. In this situation, the provider has an impossible, or at least a very discouraging task. As Peter Drucker says: "information specialists . . . . can no more manage data for users than a personnel department can take over the management of the people who work with executives."[4] Drucker also suggests that few executives know how to ask for or articulate what information they need to do their jobs.

The point is that most of the learning, training, and discussion by those in the "intelligence" industry has been supply side–oriented and focused on the intelligence process from a theoretically ideal provider's view, rather than on the demand side reality of the user's perspective and practice. The problem may indeed be with the users. But the source of the problem resides with the intelligence provider and what has been fed (or has not been fed) to the provider that has caused the problem of user indigestion. This chapter will address some additional supply side issues and opportunities for the provider that are related to missing links in the system and suggest some new or further initiatives to overcome demand side impediments to a formal intelligence program.

Problems and issues that continue to plague the provider who is interested in efforts to professionalize and legitimize formal intelligence can be grouped under five headings:[5]

1. Organizational location of the intelligence function
2. Provider expertise and interest
3. Overlapping and conflicting information sources
4. "Image" problems
5. Understanding the user's agenda

Dealing with and resolving these related problems and issues is an essential requirement for providing credible, valued, and usable intelligence products to users and in developing a subsequent user commitment and enthusiasm for the intelligence program.

ORGANIZATIONAL LOCATION

Competitive intelligence appears to be primarily located within three major organizational functions: marketing, engineering, and planning, with marketing as the dominant location. Of course, the intelligence function can be located elsewhere and sometimes is the responsibility of the corporate or business library or a separate competitive or business intelligence unit. The 1989 Society of Competitive Intelligence Professionals survey not only identifies these locations but also provides support for the obvious corollary. That is, the intelligence purpose in these functional areas is to support the function. In one major telecommunications company, the intelligence goal is to collect and process information to support marketing strategies and plans. Seventy-five percent of user requests for information are from the marketing and product management departments. The problem for the intelligence provider is not necessarily the location of the intelligence program, but is more likely the intended, or possibly unintended, result of having the intelligence beginnings in marketing or engineering.[6] The problem in the case of a marketing-based intelligence effort really has two dimensions: (1) domain—marketing box only—an extension of market research linked to the marketing environment; and (2) linkages/network—only with marketing function managers, and not with other managers and decision-makers who are stakeholders in marketing plans and actions (legal, purchasing, manufacturing, the CEO, etc).

The intelligence initiative is often an evolution of market research or reverse engineering or benchmarking or some other functional activity that is already in place. It is an add-on responsibility for people who are primarily engaged in the usual or traditional functional activity. A marketing function may be an ongoing activity in many parts of the organization—defense, consumer, European, or fiber optics marketing. Each of these marketing operations may be linked by common customers, suppliers, processes, or competitors. But the consumer marketing intelligence in this example is not linked to any of these other common market interests, needs or domains. It is invisible to others in the organization whose support and commitment to a formal intelligence program would serve to credibly legitimize the program.

In this not uncommon situation, the intelligence provider has three options to consider that can be directed toward improving and overcoming the generic intelligence impediments of credibility, value, and utilization by senior managers in the organization.

1. If there is, for example, a manager in the consumer electronic marketing group who sees real value in the intelligence product and enthusiastically supports the process, and has credible relationships with senior managers in other areas or functions, this person can lead the effort to spread the good news—the intelligence gospel. The group manager who might

be the missionary salesperson must be strongly motivated to play this role. That is, playing the role of missionary or champion will serve to benefit this manager in some way—recognition, a "team player," or promotion. The missionary manager must be credibly seen as a true believer in intelligence and be able to convince others of the benefits of an intelligence program.

2. The intelligence provider can play the missionary role. This initiative would require that the provider has group credibility, a positive track record, and a network outside the group. The provider can meet formally or informally with other information providers or users. The risks here can be associated with "going around the boss" or "meddling" and of course, missionary or initiative failure that can be damaging both professionally and personally to the group intelligence provider.

3. The group intelligence provider can arrange to be transferred to a more visible and influential group that would benefit by this additional intelligence resource and asset. Obviously, there is personal risk in this approach. It also requires the endorsement of someone else in the group *and* an outstanding provider record of accomplishment by the provider. A request for transfer (or applying for a new position with another group) carries the risk of being viewed by the group as "traitorous" behavior.

Although the first option is probably more realistically possible and the better option, it is more likely that once the intelligence function is established within marketing or engineering or wherever, it will stay there. It will thus have limited, if any, effect on the need to build user demand for "intelligence" among senior managers and decision-makers. This dismal but real probability is related to a second problem area.

PROVIDER EXPERTISE AND INTERESTS

The term "intelligence professional" is in practically all cases inappropriate and optimistically misleading. Intelligence will not be a profession until there is both a common acceptance of what intelligence means and its essential purpose as defined by intelligence users.[7] There must be an agreed-upon body of knowledge and experience appropriate to the professionalization of intelligence, as, for example, there is in law, medicine, or accounting. Until this happens, the intelligence providers are not and will not be considered professionals. The fact that the SCIP includes the word "professional" in its title may signify noble intent but is not yet reality. We can agree that government intelligence officers with years of training and experience, who have found new careers in business, are in fact professionals. In the corporate intelligence industry with its estimated ten thousand or so intelligence providers (this figure has been used by several competitive intelligence consultants, but cannot be verified in part because of a lack of agreement on the domain and scope of intelligence and therefore who is really doing what that might be intelligence related), former government intelligence officers are in the minority. Further, there is no research or evidence to support an assumption that government experience can be effectively applied or utilized in the private sector. The culture, organization, environment, conditions, and purposes are significantly different in government to at least raise doubts and questions about direct and effective application in business.

However arguably the word "professional" can be attached to former government intelligence officers now in private sector intelligence (these intelligence providers *do* tend to bring a rigorous discipline to a competitive intelligence program), this leaves the significant majority of intelligence providers with limited or no professional qualifications. Most often, providers are younger and more inexperienced in business, the industry, or their organization than are the managers they are supposed to provide with useful products for planning and decisions. Providers may have a broad academic background in economics, political science, or business administration and possess good analytical or quantitative skills, but they have not been prepared for intelligence responsibilities. Many have attended intelligence seminars, workshops, and conferences and have a good sense of the theoretical processes of intelligence. With this new knowledge and renewed interest in competitive intelligence, they find it difficult to understand why their businesses don't attach the same interest or importance to a more formal or effective intelligence program.[8] As Jan Herring of the Futures Group has said when he talks about the need for corporate intelligence efforts, "it amazes me that people in the private sector haven't figured this out yet."

The focus of intelligence training is on process rather than appropriate products for the user that flow from the process. Users-customers care little if they care at all about the process, but care a great deal about the resultant product that is wanted, needed, valued, and that can be used. The industry is process-oriented or, in marketing terms, fascinated with what the product is (assessed and valuable information) rather than what the product does; value-added and credible information that the user needs and wants. This preoccupation with what the product is, is not uncommon in new industries, services, or technologies. The VCR was introduced to the U.S. market by Sony in 1976. In succeeding years, it became more complex and feature-driven to the extent that some 75 percent or 80 percent of VCR owners only use one option—play of a prerecorded tape. It was not until 1990, fourteen years after the product introduction, that some effort was made to provide a more user friendly model that most users wanted. It took more than a decade to shift the industry's preoccupation with what the product is to what the product does in terms of benefits for the user. This focus on process (as the product) is part of the reason that intelligence providers find limited and stable demand for an excess of intelligence supply—a demand bottleneck.[9]

A related reason for the limited demand for formal intelligence programs is that over a period of time, lack of a growing, enthusiastic support and commitment for a formal intelligence program does not encourage intelligence providers to think of "intelligence" as an attractive business career or "fast track" assignment. Intelligence providers, unless they are responsible on a full-time basis for the intelligence program, which is favorably viewed as a high priority and visible business resource, will shortly realize that there are better career opportunities elsewhere. Intelligence providers often have intelligence as a part-time, peripheral responsibility, which is reflected in the low level of management interest and support for a formal intelligence program that will have continuity and longevity.

The conclusion is that unless and until intelligence providers can acquire the necessary professional training and skills, learn how to focus on and deal with demand side (user) needs and values, and find some reasonable career satisfaction in an intelligence function, the problems associated with a lack of credibility, value, and usefulness on the part of users will remain a problem.

The problem results in a continuing constraint to the further development and growth of formal intelligence programs. This is not a catch 22 situation as might be suggested. Lack of user support, commitment, and demand is clogging the supply lines. But the intelligence supply side industry has created this problem by rushing products to market that users do not understand, value, and use. It is the supply sider's responsibility to change its focus and orientation to favorably reposition competitive intelligence and to favorably differentiate the intelligence program products from those of competitors.

COMPETING INFORMATION SOURCES

Senior managers have a variety of information sources to choose from in formulating plans and making decisions. Many sources are chosen because they reduce risks for the planner/decision-maker. Trusted friends and colleagues, technical experts, outside industry analysts, consultants, and, of course, the planner/decision-maker are among these lower-risk, competing sources. These sources are known, have credibility, are reliable and trustworthy, and add value for the decision-maker. Their advice, assessments, and information can thus be used with relatively minimal risks. The formal functional intelligence provider is often unknown to the user. The provider is at a level low enough in the organization to make the provider's credibility and the product's reliability questionable. Even if the provider is known to the user, the user still has other competing information or intelligence sources for choices and as options for problem solving and decision-making.

Competitive intelligence has been absorbed by other organizational information functions and activities. It is part of something else—marketing or planning or sales or some other informational service. It has never really had a life of its own. It has no institutional image as a known, independent function. It is a discrete function with which managers and information users have little if any experience. It has, at best, a neutral or nonimage, although perception of the word "intelligence," as suggested, can be quite negative. There is no positive evidence that has been shared among U.S. corporations, that formal intelligence programs have been winners. There is no public evidence that intelligence has saved the day or made any organization more profitable or competitive. The real success stories, if any, are well-kept organizational secrets. They usually aren't discussed outside the intelligence group. This can lead those outside the group to conclude that there may not be any real success stories. Even worse, there may have been mainly intelligence failures that, of course, the group is reluctant to publicize. There is obvious reluctance to talk about failures, to project less than a positive image.

A positive image is a powerful competitive advantage. For formal intelligence programs to gain this advantage, they must have an identity that is distinct from all other competing sources of intelligence. To have a separate and distinct identity, intelligence enthusiasts and staffers must offer a better product and service that is favorably differentiated by the user from the competition. The key, once again, is understanding what the intelligence customer wants, needs, and values, and then meeting the user's needs or even exceeding those needs and requirements.

The point is obvious. Unless and until intelligence providers find a way to favorably differentiate themselves and their programs from their competitors', they will remain at a competitive disadvantage.[10] The general focus of this book is on developing competitive advantages for and from formal intelligence programs. While in the long run, these advantages must be real, they must also be perceived by the users as reflecting *their* reality, *their* perceptions, *their* images of intelligence or information needs and uses.

IMAGE

In every organization or activity there is a perceived image, sometimes called reputation, which is identified with the activity and associated with the products, processes, and people that are part of the activity, and the nature of the activity or organization itself. These associations are not equally important, nor are the images of the associated parts of the activity necessarily the same. These images are held by those associated with the activity and by those outside the organization or activity: employees and customers or the IRS and taxpayers. It is interesting to observe that for the past eleven years, some three hundred major U.S. corporations have had their reputations rated and ranked by *Fortune* in its annual survey, "America's Most Admired Corporations." There are eight attributes of reputation that form the basis for the scores and rankings.[11] The pharmaceutical company, Merck, rates number one in the top three companies in most of the attributes and for the past several years has been the most admired company in the survey. Merck's products, operations, and service image are very good. It has developed and sustained this good image through years of constant small improvements—incremental changes that benefit its customers, employees, and shareholders. Merck is also a very profitable company. Its ten-year average total return to investors is well above average for all businesses and above those of its industry competitors. It may be that because a good image or reputation is the result of doing the right things right, hundreds or thousands of things, over an extended period, that image is a very powerful if not the best source of competitor advantage. This advantage is not easily copied. Perhaps not coincidentally, Merck has been reported to have a very good formal competitive intelligence program.

The point for providers is simply this. There is no "quick fix" for developing credibility, value-added, and utilization within the organization for a formal competitive intelligence program. It takes a long-term commitment to such a program by senior managers and decision-makers. The catch, which is really the thrust of this chapter, is that to gain this necessary long-term support and commitment, the intelligence provider has to do many right things right. This is not easy, but the payoff, if recognition of competitive intelligence as a key organizational resource is the payoff goal, is enormous. In concluding this brief discussion of the problem and opportunity that image presents, it is useful to consider a key element of intelligence image: ethics—specifically, the perceived ethics of intelligence.

The issue of ethics in competitive intelligence is one of importance to intelligence providers. It is important because unlike market, financial, or other commonly used business information systems, competitive intelligence is associated by the interested business public, business publications, and some managers with spying, espionage, or similar perceptions of illegal, clandestine, covert, or unethical activity. "Spies Like Us" (*Corporate Computing*), "Corporate Espionage and the New KGB" (*Access Control*), "As Red Menace Cools, Spies Go Corporate" (*Wall Street Journal*), "The Sting" (*Wall Street Journal*), "Corporate Spies Snoop to Conquer" (*Fortune*), "007 It's Not, But Intelligence Is In" (*New York Times*), "Competitor Intelligence Comes in from the Cold" (*Across the Board*), "The New Face of Japanese Espionage" (*Forbes*), "Spying on the Competition: Costly Benefits" (*Wall Street Journal*), and "How to Snoop on Your Competitors" (*Fortune*), are some examples of articles that fuel this public perception. The reasons for these perceptions are almost self-evident, residing in the legacy of national intelligence agencies and their portrayal in news, books, films, and academic approaches to college and university intelligence programs. Businesses, which often have a corporate code of ethics that is published, communicated, and reaffirmed annually by employees, are naturally reluctant to associate too closely with this legacy. Intelligence providers thus have an image problem to overcome if their function and programs are to be accepted and to have credibility with senior managers and intelligence users. The Society of Competitive Intelligence Professionals tries to help overcome this problem with its own code of ethics, which is to be acknowledged and followed by its members in their business and consulting activities. Consultants often have their own code of ethics. Additionally, businesses and business vendors may also have ethical codes for software, products and services, purchasing, and so on.

While ethics or ethics statements are talked about and posted throughout various levels and functions of the organization, the various codes may not be entirely consistent or complementary.[12] In any event, there are often mixed signals being received by intelligence providers as to what code is important to whom. Further, the degree of congruence between personal and organizational values and expected behavior may shift and change as economic, competitive, or personal events occur and change. Ethics for intelligence providers pose similar conflicts and risks for the individual as do any other institutionally derived codes. Providers must find ethical guidelines that meet the realities of the organization and expectations of its managers. Providers need to discuss and learn more about the ethical conflicts and risks, means of resolution, and importantly, seek to raise the credibility of the corporate intelligence function with the intelligence users as suggested in this and other chapters.

THE USER'S AGENDA

The starting point, as has been indicated and stressed many times in this book, is with those key managers and decision-makers who want and need information to help their planning and action decisions. The user's agenda includes not only those factors suggested in Chapter 4, but the problem areas of organizational location, provider credibility, and competing information sources that in the aggregate help convey an image or reputation of the formal competitive intelligence program to the CEO. This is a classic market or customer research problem that must be addressed by the provider. Intelligence providers have a major responsibility to profile their users. They can also use and benefit with some help from the industry's supporting cast of consultants, academics, and the intelligence society. (Utilizing this infrastructure to develop the needed credibility, value, and utilization of formal competitive intelligence efforts is discussed in Chapter 9.)

It is worth noting again that research concerning corporate intelligence programs is almost nonexistent. Research concerning both supply and demand side issues is necessary to fine tune the many assumptions concerning the products and processes of intelligence that have been proposed. This requirement, however, is not an excuse or reason for not taking some actions along with the associated risks, now.

The preceding chapters have focused on and stressed the importance of creating demand side intelligence interest. Chapters 6, 7, and 8 present and discuss useful and additional initiatives that can be applied by intelligence providers in overcoming some of the demand side obstacles and in creating more useful competitor profiles. In the aggregate, these eight chapters suggest ways to further strengthen the intelligence provider efforts to differentiate formal intelligence programs from those of competitors and to provide reliable, credible, value–added, and usable products and services for the CEO.

NOTES

1. While Reimann, a professor of management at Cleveland State University, in the *Fortune* article, November 2, 1992, 104, "The New Race for Intelligence," makes an excellent point, the "new whole" is that which is important to the intelligence user for a particular reason or need and not just the result of an interesting supply side process of creating intelligence. The entire article, as is the usual case, focuses on how to do it rather than the missing links of why, what, how and when that are related to the user's needs, wants, and interests.

2. Ibid.

3. "The Largest Survey of 'Leading Edge' Competitor Intelligence Managers," by John E. Prescott and Daniel C. Smith, *Planning Review*, May–June 1989. In Exhibit 8 of this article, respondents to the survey indicated that among the problems associated with competitive intelligence programs were: managers not aware of CI purpose (28%), limited interaction with end users (28%), no champion for CI activities (27%), and managers not using CI provided to them (16%).

4. "Be Data Literate—Know What to Know: Drucker on Management," *Wall Street Journal.* December 1, 1992.

5. Marvin Ott in his article, "Reform Task for Woolsey at the CIA," *Wall Street Journal*, December 23, 1992, suggests another group of three problems facing the CIA analyst: (1) politicization, (2) bureaucratization, and (3) a disconnect between intelligence and policy–making. He goes on to say that "most analysts are given scant sense that their work is relevant to policy. They get little or no feedback from policy makers and seldom have contact with policy officials."

6. The Conference Board report on competitive intelligence (1988) indicates that managers find information related to pricing, sales data, new products and product mix, advertising/marketing

activities, and key customers/markets to be about 75 percent of the most useful information needed. This suggests that in many organizations, competitive intelligence is really market/marketing intelligence. *Information Week*, March 23, 1992, in a business intelligence article, suggests that a first step in building a business intelligence system is to establish an alliance with the marketing department.

7. The question of whether "competitor intelligence professionals constitute a profession" was the theme of Professor L. Fahey's keynote address at the 1990 SCIP annual conference. His address is summarized in the *Competitive Intelligence Review*, vol. 1, no. 1, Summer 1990.

8. In Ghoshal's and Westney's article, the authors cite two principal impediments to effective competitor analysis: lack of relevance of outputs to actions and credibility problems. They also state that research concerning competitor analysis in the corporate context has been virtually nonexistent.

9. "The (information) overload resulted, not from any lack of information, but from its lack of quality and from the senior decision maker's lack of ability to evaluate it" (Fess Crockett, 39, "Revitalizing Executive Information Systems," in the *Sloan Management Review*, Summer 1992.

10. A source for intelligence providers interested in opinions about managing information services and in greater awareness concerning the competition for intelligence sources available to users, may wish to refer to *The Conference Board* Report Number 1020, "Managing the Future of Information Service," 1993.

11. These eight attributes of reputation are:

- *Quality of Management*
- *Use of Corporate Assets*
- *Financial Soundness*
- *Value as Long-Term Investment*
- *Quality of Products or Services*
- *Innovativeness*
- *Ability to Attract, Develop, and Keep Talented People*
- *Community and Environmental Responsibility*

12. Ethical codes concerning the collection of information about

competitors may be the exception rather than the rule. The *Financial Times* of January 22, 1993, reported on a study of American codes of conduct by Professor L. S. Paine of the Harvard Business School faculty. Paine found that "fewer than 12 out of 480 companies gave any real guidance to employees on methods for gathering competitive intelligence." *Harvard Business School Bulletin*. April 1993, 22.

PART TWO

ADDING VALUE

Chapter 6

Intelligence and Counterintelligence

Counterintelligence: The protection of an organization's own plans, actions, resources, and intelligence capabilities from the actions of another organization's intelligence activities.

This definition is generally the classical and common one for government counter-intelligence services. Some of the elements of a counterintelligence program as described by A. N. Shulsky in *Silent Warfare*[1] include denying information to others, security programs, actions taken to identify and prevent an adversary's agents (spies or moles) from obtaining and using sensitive information, and taking steps to counter deceptive or misleading information initiated and disseminated by an adversary. At first blush, it might appear that the classical and common meaning of counterintelligence is not directly applicable or appropriate to businesses and other nongovernment organizations. After all, business managers probably do not believe in or worry a great deal about competitors' spies, sleepers, or moles penetrating their organization and intelligence system and for good reasons. Most organizations do not have a formal competitive or competitor intelligence program. And as so much information about businesses is readily available in the public domain, there is little if any need for a competitor to engage in illegal, covert, or espionage actions. And, of course, the rules of the game for government intelligence services and corporations are quite different. Or, are they?

Table 6.1

ECONOMIC ESPIONAGE

Recent cases of known and suspected government-sponsored industrial espionage.

1991

- French intelligence agents working undercover as staff in the Nikko Hotel, Paris, broke into two rooms of visiting executives of the National Cash Register Co., making off with two lap-top computers believed to contain valuable corporate secrets.

- After losing a major contract to a European competitor, a large American electronics firm examining the winning bid found an exact copy of its pricing proposal and realized that its communications were being intercepted by a foreign intelligence service that supplied the information to the competitor.

- Two men were spotted stealing bags of trash from outside the home of a U.S. computer executive in Houston in a search for corporate secrets. One of the men was the French consul in Houston.

- A U.S. company found that Salvadoran workers recruited by a foreign spy service had planted electronic transmitters on computer keyboards to obtain company secrets.

- Intelligence-gathering ships of the former Soviet navy have turned their electronic ears on the telephone conversations of American businessmen to obtain economic intelligence.

Table 6.1 cont'd

1987

■ French intelligence planted several moles within the executive levels of three overseas American companies. Until they were uncovered in 1989, the corporate double agents stole valuable trade secrets and passed them to France's government–owned computer firm, Compagnie des Machines Bull.

1986

■ Israeli agents stole commercially valuable spy camera technology from Recon/Optical Inc., an Illinois optics firm, as part of an economic espionage operation.

Source: Washington Times. February 9, 1992.

Table 6.2

EYE ON SPYING

Foreign intelligence services use any method possible, from the low–tech to the very highest of high–tech, to intercept secrets of U.S. businesses and give them to competitors. Some typical examples of how it works:

Low–Tech

1. Identify personnel with access to information—anyone from business executive to hotel janitor.

2. Bribe the key personnel to become agents.

3. Agents find and retrieve information, possibly sifting through trash or stealing a briefcase from a hotel room.

Table 6.2 cont'd

Low–Tech

4. Agents turn information over to foreign intelligence service.

5. Intelligence service passes data to foreign rival of U.S. firm.

High–Tech

1. Foreign intelligence service rents office near targeted U.S. firm—car manufacturer, communications firm, etc.

2. Sophisticated electronic listening posts are set up in the office and manned round the clock.

3. Bribed personnel within the targeted firm plant sophisticated listening devices on or near electronic communications devices.

4. Listening posts eavesdrop on telephone, fax, telex, and computer communications.

5. All intercepted communications are fed into computers.

6. Computers sift through material for valuable data.

7. Intelligence service passes data to foreign rival of U.S. firm.

Source: Washington Times. February 9, 1992.

Figure 6.1

HIGH-TECH THEFT

Results of survey conducted last year by the American Society for Industrial Security Standing Committee on Safeguarding Proprietary Information. A total of 165 U.S. corporations took part.

Has your firm experienced theft or attempted theft of proprietary information or unauthorized use of technology by domestic or foreign entities?

Yes: 61
37%

No: 104
63%

Those involved in thefts:

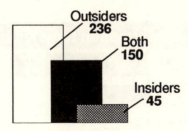

Outsiders
236

Both
150

Insiders
45

Figure 6.1 cont'd

HIGH-TECH THEFT

Types of technologies targeted:

- Semiconductor design
- Software development
- Chemical process technology
- Integrated circuits
- Security technology
- Medical technology
- New product development
- Aerospace
- Electronic banking
- Pharmaceutical
- Electro-mechanical
- Optics
- Packaging
- Telecommunications

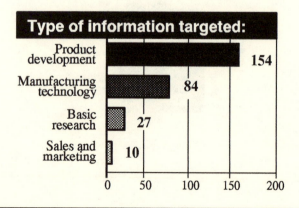

Type of information targeted:

Type	Value
Product development	154
Manufacturing technology	84
Basic research	27
Sales and marketing	10

Figure 6.1 cont'd

HIGH-TECH THEFT

■ Removal of information from offices

■ Theft of customer lists

■ Theft of technical data

■ Bribery

■ Unauthorized reproduction of documents

■ Electronic interception of fax and telephone communications

---

■ Use of foreign engineers posing as visiting trainees who looted materials and information

---

■ Former employees who stole information upon leaving and contacted competitors

---

■ Installation of microphones and eavesdropping transmitters

■ Theft of executive luggage

"The pharmaceutical industry has been screaming bloody murder about this [kind of case] and they're losing an awful lot of trade secrets."

Source: Washington Times. February 9, 1992.

Tables 6.1 and 6.2, and Figure 6.1 suggest that competitors are indeed interested in obtaining each other's "secrets" and are willing to and do employ a variety of questionable and unusual means, from the perspective of business managers and enterprises, to obtain information. There are numerous examples of competitors successfully penetrating an organization and obtaining vital information. Here are a few from the past three years.

Inside Threats and Outside Threats

- Defectors   "High–Tech Firm Cries Trade Secret Theft."
  Wall Street Journal, October 8, 1992

  "How the FBI Snared Two Scientists Selling Drug Company Secrets."
  Wall Street Journal, September 5, 1991

- Spies   "As Cold War Fades, Some Nations' Spies Seek Industrial Secrets."
  Wall Street Journal, June 1991

  "Foiling the New Corporate Spy."
  Security Management, September 1992

  "How a Spy for Boeing and His Pals Gleaned Data on Defense Plans."
  Wall Street Journal, January 15, 1990

  "America's Cup to Scuttle Spy Tactics for 1995."
  The New York Times, April 25, 1993

- Customers   "As Piracy Grows, the Software Industry and Employees Counterattack."
  The New York Times, November 8, 1992

- Espionage   "An Israeli Contract with a U.S. Company Leads to Espionage."
  Wall Street Journal, January 17, 1992

  "Corporate Espionage and the New KGB."
  Access Control, September 1992

The point is that while competitors may not be after information about *intelligence* capabilities, they are clearly interested in obtaining information about capabilities, resources, and market advantages. Thus, counterintelligence defined more broadly as measures taken to prevent a competitor from gaining information or knowledge that would give that competitor an advantage is applicable and appropriate in the corporate domain. The term "corporate security" may appear to be analogous to or much the same as counterintelligence. Corporate security programs are intended to prevent unauthorized access to sensitive areas of physical property and information and to discourage loose lips or leaks. However, this term should be abandoned or included in a broader counterintelligence program for two reasons.

First, continuing use of the term, "corporate security", is a powerful incentive to continue to think of safeguarding an organization's advantages in traditional ways. Uniformed security personnel checking badges and locks, nondisclosure agreements, and corporate campaigns to educate employees concerning the hazards of talking about what they do or about company matters with those outside the company come to mind. This pattern of thinking should change as the competitive environment is changing. An impediment to change is the conventional terminology. Second, protecting a corporation's asset and resource advantages is a technical and human challenge.[2] It is a problem that extends well beyond the traditional corporate security domain. On the other hand, what the protective program is called or titled is less important than considering what the protective program should be and what it is intended to protect. Counterintelligence may or may not be an appropriate term, depending on the perceived image and interpretation of the term. While terminology can either blunt or sharpen thinking about this matter, for most companies operating in industries that are characterized by new technologies, new products, or first to market competitive advantages, protection of these advantages is at least as important as is security for an organization's competitive intelligence activities.

Counterintelligence is an important and value–added component for competitive intelligence positioning and programs. Presently, the purpose of a counterintelligence program in terms of domain and intent of a program, and system users and provider initiatives has yet to be considered or defined. There are three issues related to this first of three value-added initiatives (the second and third initiatives are discussed in Chapters 7, 8, and 9):

• What assets, resources, and information should be protected?
• How could what is to be safeguarded be penetrated?
• Should counterintelligence be part of a formal competitive intelligence program?

The question of what should be safeguarded or protected is not easily answered. On the one hand is the operational need and market advantage of sharing information with other business units, customers, suppliers, distributors, the press and, sometimes, competitors. It is often advantageous to share information about those products, processes, and developments that are thought to enhance the market or business position of the organization. These might include R&D initiatives, process technology, quality and cost improvements, and so on. In some competitive situations, it may seem advantageous to disclose new plans or operations as a means of signaling intentions to the market or competitors.[3] However, because so much information concerning an organization's plans and operations must be filed with regulatory and government agencies, much of this kind of information is readily available in the public domain. Information in this case can be controlled but not denied. On the other hand, most competitors would find it interesting and perhaps useful to know more about an organization's thinking and decision-making that results in planning and actions that in turn result in investments and allocation of resources. This kind of information and the results of using this information are often linked to potential sources of competitive advantage for the organization. Thus, these "intellectual" property resources should be safeguarded on a need to know basis. As a formal competitive intelligence program is a potentially significant source of competitive advantage, information about this resource should also be safeguarded. Different organizations will differ in their views of what is really the source or sources of advantage for the organization. But in general, information that is important enough to protect should be linked with a source of advantage, which is the generic answer to the question of why protect it. And inevitably, this information is not compromised by machines, budgets, technology, or products, but by people—by loose lips and by those who will indulge in the universal propensity to talk about what they do and what they know.

People like to tell others about what they do, their accomplishments, and their work. It is not realistically possible to change this fundamental human characteristic, no matter how many buttons, brochures, or security seminars are made available to employees of the corporation. The best that can be done is really a two-step approach to safeguarding information that is considered to be of importance to the firm. First, identify those truly important organizational sources of advantages. These are advantages that if obtained by a competitor could erode that advantage and result in loss of an important contract, customer defections, or loss of market leadership. The net result would adversely affect the resource strength and position of the organization. Second, identify those in the organization who know what the *intent* of the source of advantage is to be when it is in place or operational. That is, what is the plan and objective in utilizing the advantage? These are the people, a manageable number, who should be oriented and motivated to not talk to others both inside and outside the organization. In fact, personal profiles of these key people, much like profiling the competition's key managers, is appropriate in terms of identifying possible security risks. If counterintelligence or corporate security is about safeguarding information that could give a competitor an advantage, then fundamentally, counterintelligence is closely associated with competitive intelligence. Both are concerned with gathering information that will be used by the organization to develop some form of competitive advantage.

Thus, the third question is largely rhetorical. A formal competitive intelligence program should include a counterintelligence function. Not only are the two activities, offensive and defensive, linked, but they also offer the competitive intelligence staff yet another avenue of opportunity to meet the intelligence user's needs and wants. Counterintelligence can be a value-added and useful product. Some will argue that "counterintelligence" is not in the domain of a competitive intelligence program, but is a separate, internal, controllable matter for management attention. Nonetheless, both are information-based and are related to risks, threats, opportunities, and advantages. Intelligence is a powerful source of advantage and counterintelligence is another form of intelligence. Counterintelligence, as contrasted to corporate secur- ity programs, is nonexistent. Its exclusion will weaken and minimize the effectiveness and value of corporate intelligence programs and investments.[4]

Finally, it should be recognized that an aggressive counterintel- ligence program in a corporate or business setting raises significant questions concerning rights to privacy in the workplace. Although employers know, and claim the right to know, a great deal about their employees—their habits, health, finance, outside interests, and how they respond to customer service calls—a serious counterintelligence effort would escalate the privacy issue. After all, counterintelligence is concerned with competitor abilities and intentions to penetrate an organization's secrets and with its ability to use this intelligence to confuse and subvert competitors' interests. The activities of enemy agents, spies, moles, and sleepers is real enough in the business world today. Counterintelligence can serve to realistically or perceptually enlarge this clandestine and subversive activity—even to the point of paranoia about who is loyal and who is not.

The point is, of course, that increasingly it would become essential to know even more about the private and public lives of our employees—at least key employees or those upon whom "suspi- cion" has been cast. There is a well-known and documented study of this phenomenon in the various articles and books that deal with counterintelligence in the CIA under its enthusiastic director, J. J. Angleton. The trade-off issues associated with the question of protecting business secrets and protecting an individual's rights to privacy is clearly raised in the August 9, 1993 *Fortune* article, 89, "What the Boss Knows about You." An excerpt from the article serves to reinforce some of the delicate points at issue: "Workplace privacy is an issue that reaches beyond employer and employee relations. Business is increasingly vulnerable to corporate espionage . . . . The employee who uses a cellular telephone is operating a mobile radio station that may inadvertently be broadcasting information to anyone within radio wave earshot." The article also indicates what employers (presently) can and cannot legally seek to know about employees. The battle between employer rights to know and employee rights to privacy on some of these and other issues (i.e., exercise and health–related habits) is being waged in the courts and in legislative debates. The article also includes a section, "Calling All Saboteurs and Swindlers," which discusses various communication coding or encryption practices, policies, and issues.

While the privacy issues are real and relevant, the corporate espionage threat is also real and relevant. The risks, rewards, and trade–offs will be evaluated differently by different businesses and industries, depending on their technological importance and perceptions of competitive threat. Nonetheless the fact that counter–intelligence is a legitimate component of a CI program, and that the combination of intelligence and counterintelligence is a powerful source of competitive advantage, provides a significant incentive to address and resolve the related questions and issues. This is a value–added initiative.

The second value–added initiative as an integral part of an effective intelligence program is personality profiling—understanding the competitor's key intelligence users, managers, and decision-makers who plan, take actions, make investment choices, and allocate resources.

NOTES

1. Shulsky (*Silent Warfare*) in Chapter 5, "Spy vs. Spy, Counterintelligence," defines counterintelligence as "information collected and analyzed, and action taken to protect a nation (and its own intelligence–related activities) against the actions of hostile intelligence services." He suggests that there should be a special office dedicated to counterintelligence analysis.

2. In *The Business Intelligence System*, Benjamin and Tamar Gilad discuss counterintelligence (p. 210–13) from the point of view of safeguarding an organization's data with physical, technical, and human measures such as educating employees and creating a reputation for toughness in combating espionage and intelligence leaks.

They do not indicate who in the organization should initiate or be responsible for a counterintelligence program and state that "industrial espionage is not business intelligence."

3. "Signaling" by competitors is usefully discussed in Porter's *Competitive Strategy*, (Chapter 4, "Market Signals") and is directly related to basic competitor analysis.

4. It is encouraging to note that the Fall 1992–Winter 1993 issue of *The Competitive Intelligence Review* contains an article on counterintelligence, "Counterintelligence: A New Business Requirement," by W. E. DeGenaro. De Genaro has professional experience in this area. It is likely that there will be further discussion and publication concerning corporate counterintelligence issues.

REFERENCES

Duggan, P., and G. Eisenstadt, "The New Face of Japanese Espionage." *Forbes,* November 12, 1990, 96.

Gilad, B. and Gilad, T. 1988. *The Business Intelligence System: A New Tool for Competitive Advantage.* New York: AMACOM.

O'Toole, G. J. A. 1991. *Honorable Treachery: A History of U.S. Intelligence, Espionage and Covert Action from the American Revolution to the CIA.* New York: Atlantic Monthly Press.

Porter, M. E. 1980. *Competitive Strategy: Techniques for Analyzing Industries and Competitors.* New York: The Free Press.

Shulsky, A. N. 1991. *Silent Warfare: Understanding the World of Intelligence.* McLean: Brassey's (U.S.).

Sigurdson, J., and P. Nelson, "Intelligence Gathering and Japan: The Elusive Role of Grey Intelligence." *International Journal of Intelligence and Counterintelligence,* vol. 5, no. 1, Spring 1991, 17–34.

Chapter 7

Competitor Profiling and Competitive Intelligence

Guns don't kill people; people kill people.

The NRA's credo is subject to debate, but an analogous observation about the corporate world is not.

Organizations don't make decisions; *people* make decisions. And insofar as it is important to know what clients and competitors are "going to do," understanding the *leaders* of those organizations is critical. The behavior of organizations cannot be anticipated solely on the basis of what they *can* do or what they *might* do. It can only be anticipated on the basis of what their leaders *are willing* to do, and this requires a realistic understanding of how these leaders—the presidents, the chairpersons, the owners, the managers, the CEOs, and the operating chiefs who call the shots, who absorb the staff studies, who make the critical decisions—make their decisions.

Are they bold or cautious? Are they frightened by risk or willing to "bet the farm"? Are they ultimately concerned about the "bottom line" or especially dedicated to the welfare of their employees?

Is their ultimate loyalty to the organization, or to themselves, or do they see these two entities as "one and the same"? Is competition a "game" in which you lose some and win some; or is it a deadly struggle in which any loss is an unbearable defeat?

These predispositions are as much a factor in the decision-making processes of individual managers as their knowledge of market forces and their assessment of their organization's capabilities. In critical cases, these "internal" factors may even transcend the combined impact of all the "objective" information that otherwise comes to bear, inhibiting a decision about an otherwise fruitful enterprise or provoking one in the face of "overwhelming odds" and "unreasonable risk."

Aware of the relevance of these factors, two of World War II's most effective ground commanders—Germany's Field Marshal Erwin Rommel and America's General George S. Patton—studied their adversaries as an integral part of their battlefield preparations. Their knowledge of how their opponents "ticked" was as much a part of their strategic preparations as their surveys of the terrain, their assessment of their respective resources, and their commitment to contingency planning. In contrast, Britain's Bernard Law Montgomery had a much more personal focus, and was an endless source of conflict within the Allied councils, because he could not subordinate his ego to the interests of collegial cooperation. Douglas MacArthur had an overarching sense of destiny, and his own role in fashioning it. The priorities and predispositions of these diverse personalities bore heavily on their behavior and their planning processes; and colleagues and adversaries were at risk if they failed to allow for them, in *their* plans and decisions.

Intelligence analysts learn early on that assessment of adversaries *intentions* deserves every bit as much attention as knowledge of their *capabilities*. The Cold War was a forty-five-year exercise in assessing and influencing the opposition's *intentions* about using their nuclear capabilities. In mounting Operation Desert Storm, vast resources had to be diverted to protection against Iraq's capacity to launch gas attacks, because of uncertainty about Saddam Hussein's *intentions* about using them (which, in fact, he did *not* do).

In a separate but related way, the tragedy at Waco, Texas, in April

1993 emerged not from an awareness of what Koresh *could* do, but from misperceptions of what he *would* do. Conventional wisdom suggested that a measured assault would be effective; but conventional wisdom is the lurking pitfall for those who formulate intelligence: "Those in charge of the Waco operation viewed David Koresh monochromatically: He was someone who had broken the law and must, in the words of one official, 'submit himself to the law.' Logical? Perhaps. But logic has nothing to do with a mind like Koresh's."[1]

When it comes to crisis management and decision-making, Koresh is not unique. In fact, he is not even unusual. *Less than a third* of the U.S. population is "wired" to make decisions on a wholly rational, logical, objective basis (whether we be managers, teachers, carpenters, or bus drivers). The rest of us are constitutionally responsive to or even controlled by values, priorities, or predispositions that play the dominant role in our critical decisions. That doesn't make us "crazy"; but it does make each of us unique, independent, individualistic, hard to predict.

Unfortunately, we are not educated to view the world from this perspective. Our training for business and management, and the disciplines of our planning processes, encourage us to focus on logic and analysis and to infer that all other managers and decision-makers do the same. Our conventional processes for analyzing the business environment—including our efforts to understand our competitors and to anticipate their pending actions—typically focus on

the market factors and history of the industry
the history and performance of the "organization of interest"
   (typically compiled in statistical or other "scientific" terms)
the "visible" history and performance of the "decision-maker"
   (typically compiled in the sterile documentation form of year
   books and obituaries)

From these—carefully sifted through the complex and disciplined processes of professional staffs—we derive or receive analyses that are painfully compiled with the most stringent professional discipline to produce scientific, objective, logical, and rational forecasts that are, by the very discipline of those processes, destined to be "off the mark" about two—thirds of the time.

As Robert J. Samuelson observes, business education and management practice over the past generation has fostered "the belief that all problems could be solved by analysis" and "favored the rise of executives who were adept with numbers and making slick presentations"; but "we recognize that *differences in talent, temperament,* knowledge and experience make some people good at some things and not at others."[2]

Those differences in talent and temperament, along with related psychological or behavioral influences, combine to produce *intentions, inclinations, or predispositions* to courses of action that are wholly unrelated to the outcomes of analysis or the products of "reason." This is the way people work--in the real world, drawing on *all* their resources and experience.

Consequently, in the corporate world, the *personal style* of individual leaders has a pronounced influence on their policies and their major decisions. These, in turn, shape the organizations they lead and establish a tone for the way they function. Frank Lorenzo displays a profound proclivity for imposing control over the organizations he acquires, even to the point of provoking confront-ation with the workforce. Donald Trump and Jack Kent Cooke show substantially less interest in the details of management (which they are content to leave to others), and relish the "game" of entrepreneurship and the attention that their actions command. Lee Iacocca and Robert Crandall show substantially broader perspec-tives; in contrast to many of their peers and competitors, they show a willingness to defer short-term interests, when necessary, in order to pursue long-term goals. Bill Gates and Steve Jobs are vision-aries, endlessly challenged by the prospect of new areas to be explored, new routes to be traveled.

So *why is personality profiling important in our efforts to understand our clients and our competitors*? Because their personal idiosyncrasies and predispositions will have a greater bearing on the critical decisions they make than a calculated assessment of their resources and capabilities. Fewer than a third of all the people who make decisions are capable of making them on a wholly dispassionate, rational basis. The overwhelming rest of us will make decisions that are shaped at least as much by fears of risk (or the challenge to take them), by the need to control events and to evade chaos, by preoccupation with our relations with others (either to take care of them, or to control them, or to curry their favor or their approval), by the pursuit of favorite goals or activities (however unrealistic they may be), or by the compulsion to salve our own egos. Most of our clients and competitors respond to these same, often "irrational" forces. Knowing what these are vastly improves our ability to anticipate what they will do.

How does this benefit us, as decision–makers and planners? It protects us from making *rational decisions*! Or, more precisely, it protects us from assuming that our clients and competitors will make *their* decisions on a wholly rational basis, objectively analyzing their own resources and market factors with the same detachment that we use in our efforts to evaluate *their* positions. It strongly enhances our ability to "walk in their shoes" as we anticipate their needs and problems. With this understanding, we substantially increase our ability to make our own corporate decisions in ways that are truly productive—either because they are cordial to the interests and needs of our clients, or because they are a "step ahead" of the competition.

What resources should an organization have, in order to "do" profiling?

Whether the task is performed as a part–time job by one person, or as a full–time function by a staff that is dedicated to that purpose, certain components are necessary to "get the job done." Someone has to decide who should be profiled, and why. With the *task* thus established, information has to be *collected* and brought to the analysts. The information has to be evaluated and *processed*. From this, a *profile* must be generated that addresses the established requirements; and this must be *reported* to management—to those who generated the requirement in the first place. As decisions are made and actions are taken, the results of these actions should be evaluated and *reported back* to the collectors and analysts, to keep track of successes and failures and, thereby, to enlighten and improve the process. In short, one or more persons must be concerned with: *Requirements; Tasking and Collection; Processing and Analysis: Profiling; Reporting; Validation and Feedback.*

Requirements. To initiate the process, someone has to decide who should be profiled among our clients and competitors, and why. Who *are* the critical clients and competitors? Who are the key decision–makers in those organizations? What decisions are anticipated in the foreseeable future that will affect the course of these organizations and, implicitly, our relations to them? (Are significant changes looming in the marketplace, to which all competitors will have to adjust? Is the organization facing a challenge to make significant changes in its product line? Has it suffered significant losses in the recent past? Is it facing significant new confrontations from its competitors?) Ideally, these questions should be levied by senior management, by the key decision–makers in the organization, who sense that the answers to these kinds of questions are critical to corporate planning.

In the early stages of introducing an organization to the values of intelligence and profiling, management may require some training in these processes. It may be necessary to propose an initial study or two, and to fashion the requirements *for* management, in order to demonstrate how the process can work and how management will benefit from it.

Tasking and Collection. Once the requirements have been set, and a candidate has been selected for profiling, the search for information begins. *Who* can provide information on the subject, based on direct personal contact? And *where* can information be obtained from more remote resources?

For *direct* collection, are there people in our organization, or who are otherwise accessible, who have had personal contact with the subject or can develop personal contact in the near future? Do we have access to people who have worked with him in the past? Can we reach colleagues or peers who can meet him at meetings, at conferences, or at leisure?

For *indirect* purposes, where can we obtain information about this person from public records? What has he written or published? What coverage has he received from the media? What is available from his own organization on tapes, videos, or promotional materials, which can give us some sense of the person "in action," in public, with his employees, as a community leader?

Processing and Analysis. Processing and analyzing this information is the heart of the profiling process, In Chapter 8, a model is presented that suggests how the information collected from direct and indirect sources can be sorted and organized in a systematic way. This, in turn, will suggest ways in which the individual is likely to respond in critical situations: how he will order his priorities, what values will dominate his approach to problems, how he will assess risk, and how these and other factors are likely to affect his decisions.

Reporting. Having generated a profile by processing the information through the model, we can address the original requirements, and report suggestions and conclusions to management.

Validation and Feedback. As our subject and his organization live through the problems envisioned in the requirements, their performance should be "tracked" by the analysts, in order to record successes and failures as a continuing guide to future collection and processing efforts.

Who should "do" profiling? What kinds of skills are required?

As we have seen, there are two kinds of tasks involved, and each requires a different talent. One task involves collecting information directly from the persons of interest—in meetings, in social contacts, at conferences of business conventions, where opportunities exist to collect information and to make observations based on direct contact. For this kind of activity, the "natural born assessors," the people who are comfortable in new social situations, people who are skilled in meeting and responding to "new contacts," make the best reporters.

Another task, collecting and processing information *about* other people, is a different matter. In this area, by definition, profiling is an analytic process, not a "contact sport." It is much like any other effort to assess other market forces, analyzing information that is obtained remotely, indirectly, usually detached from the person of interest. Accordingly, the "good assessors," people who are "good with others," people who have a "good feel" for others, people who can respond spontaneously and successfully in social exchanges, are *not* necessarily good at the indirect, remote assessment process. Such people are denied their own natural "inputs" and resources when they have to deal with data and "reports about people," rather than with the "real person." The best profilers are likely to be people who are interested in others, but who have some measure of uncertainty about their own social skills, and who have thus spent their lives "sizing people up" in a studious way before entering into direct contact with them. This is an activity for people who would rather "analyze" other people, than deal with them "up close and personal."

PUTTING IT TOGETHER

To understand what our living, breathing, functioning, real-life competitors will do and how they will go about making the decisions that will affect their organizations, we have to achieve an understanding in four related areas.

First, we must understand the characteristics of the industry in which the manager operates and comprehend the range of movement that is possible. A profitable and growing industry will allow for different kinds of management (and tolerate a broader range of options) than a mature and marginally profitable industry.

Second, the competitor's company or organization will influence his behavior, even as he endeavors to make changes of his own. Its past performance, its traditional style, its corporate environment will all have a strong influence on how a manager thinks and what he can do. Even a new manager, brought in from the outside with a mission for change, must contend with the past and the legacies it has entrenched—if only to struggle against them. (Those who believe in opportunities for unlimited change might contemplate the experiences of Bill Clinton and his predecessors.)

Third, his own performance and track record will provide valuable clues to how he has approached various problems in the past.

Profiling provides the basis for understanding how individual predispositions will affect his own evaluation of his options—and the extent to which logical analysis will prevail—or be modified or even preempted by other factors.

Finally, as the author of this book was the first to suggest and recognize the value of personality profiling in the business competitive intelligence system, I am including one of his early articles on profiling that was written in 1992. It appeared as a chapter in the book *Global Perspective on Competitive Intelligence,* published in 1993 by the Society of Competitive Intelligence Professionals.

PROFILE ASSESSMENT: A MISSING LINK IN COMPETITIVE INTELLIGENCE
WALTER BARNDT
School of Management, The Hartford Graduate Center

Procter and Gamble, under its CEO Edwin Artzt, is changing. Artzt is making acquisitions, threatening divestitures, cutting new product spending, and cleaning out managers. P&G is changing because Artzt is making changes and because he has a vision of the game that is different than his predecessors. The rules change and it is likely that both P&G's competitors and employees are trying to figure the meaning of these changes and the "solution." The games and the players are inseparable as professional sports organizations and government intelligence agencies well know.

Indeed, in business there is a well documented history of assessing, in very formal and quantitative ways, personalities that are of interest to the business—customers and employees. Many businesses know a great deal about their customers' values and employees' skills and character. But there is a critical area of business where "profiles" of personalities are absent, relative to the interest, attention, and techniques that are usually focused on customers and employees. That area is competitors.

I do not mean to imply that companies don't analyze competitors. Many have formal "business intelligence" functions within the organizational structure that employ people to collect, analyze, and distribute competitor intelligence to the organization's decision-makers. Competitor analysis or business intelligence is a hot topic. It is a growth industry, which is apparent from the proliferation of "intelligence" consultants, articles, books, seminars, and, of course, the rapid growth of a new professional society devoted to competitive intelligence. The focus of this industry and its component parts has in my view, been limited if not myopic. It is concerned with assets, resources, property, market share, ratios, and percentages. This is important as it defines what a competitor can do and helps to forecast a competitive strategy. But it is incomplete.

It does not include the "players"; the key decision-makers who determine what to do with the assets and resources. This is the missing link; the key people in the competitor's business who should be profiled along with the R&D spending, patent applications, and customer service.

Thus, most competitor intelligence activity is incomplete. Therefore, it is also myopic. What we want from the intelligence process is a better understanding of what our competitors can and will do. We want to know about decisions and changes as the end product, not plant capacity and liquidity. We have the intelligence product definition reversed and therefore the process is only 50 percent effective or complete.

How can the analyst initiate a profile assessment? Why is the link missing, what are the benefits of adding a personal profile assessment to our intelligence efforts, and what can be done to improve the intelligence product? These are the key questions I shall try to address in this chapter.

PROFILE ASSESSMENTS

It is important to note that a profile of a competitor's decision-maker or key decision-influencer, while interesting in itself, provides only a partial indication of what the CEO, or head of R&D, or product/market development manager, or whoever is to be targeted, can and will do. A personal profile analysis has three parts. The first part is a "personality" profile. To be effective as a critical element of competitor analysis product (the competitor intelligence that is actionable), a personal profile analysis process must also be concerned with two additional information areas: the structure and characteristics of the industry in which the competitor's business performs, and the characteristics of the competitor's business. An analysis of these two areas will suggest certain historical reasons and motivations for the "opposing players'" actions and performance, and thus, what might be anticipated in the future.

Sources of information about an industry and companies within that industry are assumed to be familiar territory to the various information collectors in your organization. I also assume that there is familiarity with the array of models available for assessing the information, industry analysis, benchmarking, and investment analysis. My focus is on the variety of sources of information and models assessing personalities and incorporating them into useful intelligence (Table 7.1).

Table 7.1

Sources of Personality Profiling

Personality	Business	Industry
• Parents	• Culture	• Structure
• Children	• Company performance	• Competition
• Spouse(s)		• Investment intensity
• Early/later interests	• Employers	
• Schools	• Position–direction	• Profitability
• Avocations	• Reporting structure	• Growth
• Lifestyle	• Major responsibilities	
• Physical characteristics	• Performance	
	• Recognition	
	• Salary/compensation	
	• Who says what about target	

There are two principal sources: primary and secondary. Primary sources include people who have worked with or for the target (or for whom the target has worked)—colleagues, customers, suppliers, and distributors. Other primary sources would include observations concerning the target's interests, avocations, and lifestyle (what kind of house, cars, boats, pets, friends, clubs, clothes, and so on interest the person).

Secondary sources include anything published about (or by) the target—high school and university year books or alumni information, local newspapers, court records, business publications, and professional journals. Photographs and handwriting samples may also be of value.

The essence of an effective personal profile analysis is to develop both a complete picture of the personality and the influence on that personality of the environments in which he or she has performed or will perform. What we are looking for are consistencies and inconsistencies, as well as answers to some of the following kinds of questions:

- What values guide decisions and actions?
- A team player or a loner?
- Whose advice is trusted? (What are sources of target's "intelligence"?)
- How credible? Reliable?
- Where in "life cycle"?
- What assumptions/beliefs does the person have concerning markets, competition, managing people/other resources, and management theories/concepts?

While there are any number of models available for assessing personality (e.g. Myers-Briggs), I would urge caution in using these "profile" models, as they may seduce the analyst into believing that one model, because it is accepted, will reveal the profile for the future. That is, it may be tempting to minimize the effect of industry characteristics and company "culture" on what the target manager can or will do. And, of course, the model profile may not be an appropriate indicator of the answer to the question that initiated the analysis in the first place. The personality profile is just an extra tool in the competitive analyst's tool kit, and should be used in conjunction with other approaches. Unfortunately, it is an under-utilized tool.

As an alternative, a matrix such as the one indicated in Figure 7.1 may be helpful in visualization of the profile, possible changes and trends, and strengths of the target related to other managers who may be evaluated.

IMPEDIMENTS TO PROFILE ASSESSMENTS

There are three major impediments that need to be overcome if we want to add the personal profile dimension to our intelligence work. Japanese and European competitors attach great importance to "knowing" key competitors as people who think and feel and who make the important decisions. They have apparently found a way to overcome these major impediments, if in their scheme of things, they existed at all. In any event, the three big hurdles are people, process, and fear.

FIGURE 7.1

Personal Profile Analysis

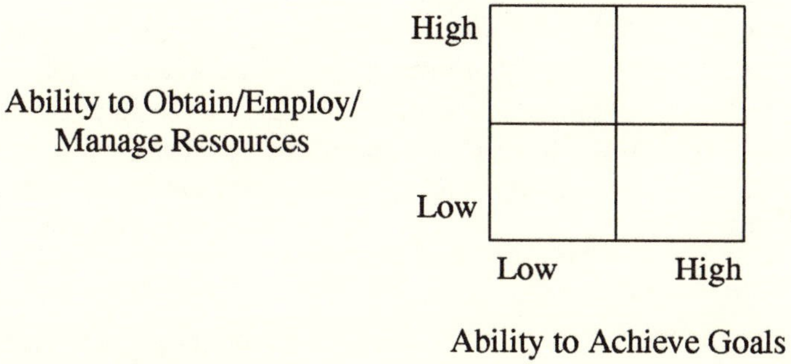

High

Ability to Obtain/Employ/
Manage Resources

Low

Low   High

Ability to Achieve Goals

The People Problem

Often, the wrong people have been given intelligence responsibilities. They are not intelligence professionals. They are marketing (research) professionals, or engineering professionals, or other traditional professionals. They can be myopic in their responsibilities because they haven't been trained or educated as professional intelligence collectors or analysts.

Their bosses (who similarly lack training) ask them to provide definite numbers and to quantitatively support their "product," and the personnel function is largely oblivious to its potential role in intelligence. Adding to the problem is the fact that there are only a handful of academics in graduate business schools who are interested in competitor analysis and offer courses in the curriculum that focus on intelligence. In *The Business Intelligence System*, the Gilads offers one paragraph in over 200 pages of systems description that suggests the value of profiling important managers and decision- makers.[3]

Process Fascination

As managers, we have been taught or have learned that things and numbers are important. Number crunching and quantification are critical. Qualitative assessments (a psychological profile of the competitor's CEO) doesn't fit. As a result, competitors tend to be viewed as impersonal and sterile, reduced to "measures" such as 10% or 35 cars per hour. Technology (computers and data bases) reinforces this perception. Our strategic planning processes are quantitatively based. We attract quantitatively oriented managers to our organizations in disproportionately larger numbers than psychologists, history majors or anthropologists. And over time, we have come to have too much faith in the numbers process, whether it is for economic forecasting, technological assessment or strategic planning.

The Fear Factor

Among the most important users of intelligence are senior managers. Senior managers protect their positions. They are suspicious of organization functions and staff who may dilute their sense of power and control. A business intelligence function, in that it collects and processes information and creates "intelligence", is one of these functions. To offset any threat, senior managers rely on their own sources of information and intelligence--people they know and can trust--including themselves. To the extent that this is a cultural characteristic of the organization, it is difficult to change. Better internal personal communications can help.

Is it worth the effort to make some changes, to lower the hurdles? Of course, if your business is seriously interested in improving the value of your intelligence effort.

value of your intelligence effort.

BENEFITS AND COSTS OF PROFILE ANALYSIS

The benefits of adding personal profile analysis to competitor analysis activity include the following:

- Improving the chances of making better plans and decisions
- Focusing employees' interest on competitors as real people who are involved in a high-stakes game
- Adding an additional source of competitive advantage
  If your competitors do not know you and you are familiar with them, that can be a potential advantage
- Giving you more confidence in the answer to your question, "What do you think X will do?"
- Helping you understand better what your business and managers *can* and *will* do
- Improving your corporate intelligence security and counterintelligence interests

There are costs attached to adding personal profile analysis, which include new costs and provider costs. From the user's, or senior manager's point of view, there will be resistance to added investment and a change in process, unless and until some added value can be anticipated. Some elaboration or examples of the suggested benefits may help. But as this may involve some substantial behavioral or perceptual change on the part of users, organizational and behavioral specialists might be usefully consulted. The cost here is not hiring consultants and reading books; it is the intangible cost of change, from the user's or customer's perspective.

On the provider or supplier side, the cost is also largely one of changed thinking about who should be responsible for intelligence—the process and the product. This means bringing different kinds of people into the organization who have real intelligence skills such as former government or military intelligence officers, investigative reporters, academics, doctoral students in the classics, or psychologists.

It is not easy to justify these changes or to prove that there is a missing link. Perhaps someone in marketing or personnel, where customer and employee assessments are acceptable and valued, can be a catalyst or an ally. Find that influential manager, whether a user or a provider, who wants to learn as well as teach.

Marshall N. Heyman

NOTES

1. Richard Restak, *Washington Post*, Sunday, April 25, 1993, C3.

2. Robert J. Samuelson, "The Death of Management," *Newsweek*, May 10, 1993, 55.

3. Gilad, B. and T., 1988, *The Business Intelligence Systems: A New Tool for Competitive Advantage*. New York: Amacom.

Chapter 8

Personality Profiling and Competitive Intelligence

Understanding Management Styles.

In the competitive intelligence process, personality profiling is a lot like preparing for a blind date. The first thing you do is find someone who knows "the target," so you can find out "What's he or she like?" You can get lots of details about hobbies and sports, how he or she does in school, what he or she likes and dislikes. But what you really want is some way to integrate all this information. You want to know, "What's he or she *like*?"

Similarly, the professional assessor strives for the sense of "being inside the individual," able to *sense* how that person feels and thinks. The assessor seeks to identify with that total person so well that he *knows* how that person will respond to circumstances, react to challenges, cope with risks, relate to other people. When the assessor has achieved that *sense*, he is ready to go to his client and say, "Okay, now I can tell you everything you want to know about George"

In the competitive intelligence environment, there are a lot of *unobservable* things that we would like to know about—a lot of areas in which we would like to make judgments, draw inferences, make projections, which we cannot derive directly from the history of the individual or the record of his own corporate experience. We find ourselves asking about unobservable, intangible, considerations like, "What are his goals? What are his (or her) motivations? What turns this person on?" In Maslow's terms, What are his interests and needs? What *can* he do? What is he *likely* to do? And, finally, what *will* he do?

We are *all* interested in achievement, in satisfactory interpersonal relationships. We *all* want success and monetary growth. We *all* like to think of ourselves as loyal individuals. But when "push comes to shove," and we have to make a choice, what comes first? When a John Sculley, as a manager, has to make changes in an organization, and to make those changes he either has to move people *out* or cut costs, what will "give"? "What socks get left out of the bag?

As one former senior manager in the government has noted:

> In my own experience as a member of a bureaucracy, I endured a great deal of pain when, because of age and experience, I had reached the point where management said, "This man should be running the activity." And I knew that *I* would make a lousy manager. Because, to be an effective manager, you have to deal with people in a reasonably objective way . . . . and I can't do that. I used to love to write fitness reports on the good people in my organization; but I used to sweat blood, trying to say something about the, frankly, lousy people in the outfit. I couldn't handle that.

The question is not whether this is good or bad. The question is, What is this guy like? And he is telling us something very important about what *this* guy is *like*.

Knowing these kinds of things is essential in trying to understand how this individual will perform under circumstances that we have not yet been able to observe, or when he finds himself in NEW circumstances, where no track record exists.

In our efforts to understand others, there are analogs we can look to for guidance in the areas of clinical psychology, counseling psychology, psychological theory, and the like. But these analogs are not well suited to this arcane task of trying to assess people in an *indirect* mode, without any *direct* access to the subject either through our own contact and observations, or by others who are professionally trained to make observations and judgments for us. It is very rare to find the opportunity to go to a John Sculley and ask, "Would you fill out the Myers–Briggs inventory for me?" In this *indirect* assessment business, circumstances rarely allow us to administer psychological tests and other conventional information collection devices in the way in which they have to be administered in order to provide valid results.

Some people approach this task by trying to fill out one of these instruments as if they were the "target person." But that is a "dangerous" activity; it is potentially very misleading (in terms of requirements of reliability and validity) because tests are developed and standardized for use on a *self*-report basis. What we obtain from using them *as if* we were the subject, is NOT necessarily how the individual is, but something about how the individual *wants* to be, or how the individual *wants to be perceived*. The better the individual is in deceiving himself and others about these desired self–images (consciously or unknowingly—and we are all trying to do that to some extent), the more error we are going to generate if we try to insert ourselves into that kind of "substitute testing" effort. We haven't learned anything about the real person; we have learned something about what he *wants* to look like.

A better procedure to use in this *indirect* assessment arena is to take *observable* information that we can collect from intermediate assets or resources and sort it through a general psychological model. We collect information from past performance, from records of what the individual has done, and from other people who have known him and worked or lived with him. Then we enter this information into a model that is based on *consistencies* in human behavior and performance. Then we use the *model* to make inferences or projections about these *otherwise unobservable* kinds of things that we are concerned about in this area of competitive intelligence, such as motivations, goals, loyalties, values, priorities, risk–taking, and other elements in the decision-making process.

And we can use it to make judgments about what the individual would do, *if*. That is what will be presented here: a *model* that lends itself to this kind of assessment, which will take us from observable behavior to judgments about unobservable motivations and probable future behavior in a management setting.

In the most general terms, such a model looks like Figure 8.1.

Figure 8.1

Inferential Profiling Model

OBSERVABLE
BEHAVIOR

UNOBSERVABLE
QUALITIES

Motivations
Loyalties
Priorities
Risk–taking
Aspirations
Crisis management
Coping with change

This model endeavors to present the elements of human behavior and psychological adjustment in a relatively simplified form. And it is designed to relate that information to the special application that concerns us here: managerial behavior in a corporate environment. Most conventional models that are developed for the purpose of explaining human behavior tend to be overly detailed for this kind of application. They aspire to deal with life experience in its entirety. They tend to treat all items of information as though they are equally important, and they try to track through life, from one phase to another, placing the same emphasis on every feature.

It doesn't work; it's overly burdensome, and it isn't necessary.

What we are presenting here is a process that uses real information in more general but more realistic terms. It should tell you *almost* everything you need to know about observing human behavior for the purpose of "entering the model." And, in turn, the model should suggest the answers to *most* questions about motivation, priorities, risk-taking, decision-making, and similar factors or considerations associated with managerial behavior.

Because the model deals with the large mass of general, mediating information, it is important that it not be taken *literally* when applying its general guidance and particular illustrations to any one individual being studied. The illustrations and exemplars that are used may suggest, for example, that "This is a masculine characteristic", or "This is a feminine characteristic", or "Most accountants are like this." These will be used to provide an understanding of the dynamics of the model, and as devices to define the characteristics and qualities that enable us to examine behavior and to classify or assign persons within the model. It doesn't follow that when you locate an individual within the model, based on the information that is available to you, that the individual is therefore masculine or feminine, or ought to be an accountant. But these descriptors should help convey some sense of the person being examined.

Here, then, is a guideline for evaluating information about people. It is a model of psychological or personality development, or behavior, or classification. We call it a "personality *and organizational* impact model," because it relates equally well to individuals and to organizations. It provides a basis not only for understanding individuals, but also the nature of organizations and the dynamics that take place within them.

AN ASSESSMENT MODEL

This model is composed of three operational *styles* and three psychological *adaptations* that govern everything that we are going to discuss. If you understand the styles and the adaptations and recognize how they come together, you have your road map for understanding and comprehending individuals, personality, human behavior, response patterns, response mechanism, and so on (see Figure 8.2).

The CORE of the model is composed of nine uniquely different and internally consistent behavioral patterns. This core is surrounded by a cluster of four patterns that are rarely found in conventional vocational or academic assessment, except as "problem cases."

These peripheral patterns are called DIVERGENT adjustments. Since it is important to be aware of them (so that you can recognize them and be aware of their implications, in case you run across them), we will describe them briefly; and then we will dismiss them from further consideration so we can focus on the core patterns that we are most likely to encounter among organizational leaders and their significant staff.

Figure 8.2

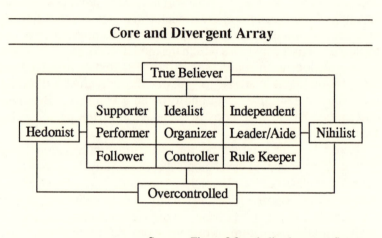

Core and Divergent Array

Source: Figure 8.2 and all subsequent figures are adapted from Saunders, Reference 4.

THE DIVERGENT CLUSTER

While they are otherwise quite different, these four divergent groups (see Figure 8.3) have certain qualities in common: they tend to be self-centered, impulsive, unpredictable, unreliable, and, in many cases, potentially volatile. At least three of the four are heavily represented among criminal populations.

True believers might well be called "bumper sticker zealots." In their search for meaning and guidance in life, they have found some leader, some cause, or some institution that they thoroughly believe in and to which they become totally dedicated. They have now found "*the answer*" to all life's problems, although they are likely to have precious little depth of understanding. Their commitment and dedication are very intense and terribly important and compelling, but it leaves them very shallow and very narrow. Their psychological well-being is dependent on their ability to accept the validity of their beliefs and the infallibility of their leaders. *Commitment* becomes more important than reason or understanding. In the ordinary course of events, they are dedicated supporters and missionaries, who are totally insensitive to "objective" analysis or criticism of their beliefs or of their leaders (since any such criticism attacks the foundations of their well-being). They are more likely to be seen as followers than as leaders; and, in the extreme, they can produce the outrages of a Jonestown mass suicide or a Waco ambuscade. If they emerge as leaders, they would tend to be hopelessly narrow and brittle.

Figure 8.3

Divergent Cluster

True Believers

Dedicated to Cause,
Belief, Group, or Leader
Blind Faith
Shallow, Overcommitted
Bumper Sticker Zealots
Tammy Bakker

Hedonist

Cool, Superficial, Hip
Charismatic
Manipulative
Superficially
Compliant
Billy Sol Estes

Self-Centered
Impulsive
Unpredictable
Unreliable
Potentially Volatile

Nihilist

Angry
Bitter
Negativistic
Reject Authority
Protesters
Charlie Manson
David Koresh

Overcontrolled

Loners
Isolated/Insulated
Brooding
Underachievers
Precipitous
John Hinckley
Bart Simpson

Hedonists are "cool," charismatic, totally self–centered, superficially compliant, and thoroughly manipulative. They are "make out" artists whose stock in trade is to "look good" and to "get away fast." Although universally attractive on brief contact, their superficiality and shallowness become apparent, sooner more often than later. In part because they are so intensely self–centered, they rarely emerge as leaders except, perhaps, among very small groups of their own kind.

The *Overcontrolled* group tend to be isolated loners. Most live out their lives in quiet and desperate isolation, showing little interest in associating with others, let alone any quest for leadership or management. Occasionally one will "snap his bonds" and thrash out in some wholly unexpected, uncharacteristic, and frightening fashion (invariably creating enormous bewilderment among casual observers who "can't believe" what this "quiet, harmless" person has done).

Nihilists are chronic and habitual protesters, in continuous war against established order, authority, or convention. They are typically very bright and very independent. While their commitment to a cause can be very intense, it is their rebelliousness that tends to characterize them. When they show up as leaders or organizers, it will most often be among dissident groups (often providing leadership for "true believers")—not as part of the Fortune 500.

THE CORE ADJUSTMENTS: THREE ADAPTATIONS

Within the CORE of the model there are three *adaptations*: an *intellectualizing*, cerebral, thinking kind of adaptation on the right side; a *feeling*, responsive, emotional, reactive adaptation on the left side; and a *balanced* group in the center. The individuals on the right tend to be *thinking*–oriented, and intellectually disciplined. Their thinking processes are essentially in command of their emotional responses. This does not mean that they have no feelings. But insofar as feelings come into play, those feelings are under the control and domination of the intellect. The individual uses feelings as an input in perceiving and analyzing.

The *"feeling"* individuals on the left side of the model like to ride on roller coasters because it is exciting and they can forget about everything else. In contrast, *"intellectualizing"* individuals who love to ride on roller coasters do it because riding on a roller coaster becomes an item of information. It creates an experience to be examined and evaluated. I've asked such people, "Don't you ever get scared?" and they say, "Of course. That's part of what it's all about." Now, *I* won't do it because I get scared, and that tells me not to do it. *They* do it, because getting scared is part of the life experience, and the "thinking" individual wants to experience these kinds of things and to contemplate them.

Figure 8.4

Core Adjustments: #1

	Right	Balanced	Left
Proactive	Supporter	Idealist	Independent
Polyactive	Performer	Organizer	Leader/Aide
Reactive	Follower	Controller	Rule Keeper

For the *"feeling"* individuals, the first response to a situation, a stimulus, an item of information, is a *feeling* response. For example, my wife will be reading TV *Weekly*, and she'll say, "They're going to have a review of the Nixon years tonight," and I'll say, "Who wants to go through *that* again" (as I clutch at my belt buckle). "Who wants to revisit that (upsetting, disturbing, aggravating) experience?" The "intellectualizing" observer is willing to revisit the experience, because "maybe they've found out something that we haven't known before." The sensing people don't want to revisit the experience because it's painful; they want to get it behind them. It's this *reaction* that comes first, and then they sort out the facts or the purposes or the values, separately and subsequently.

■ Several years ago, a couple was returning from an overseas assignment. They set about the inevitable task of buying a new car. After carefully and systematically evaluating all of their new family needs, it was obvious that what they needed was a station wagon. After visiting half the dealerships in town, they called us up on a Saturday afternoon and said, "We've got it, we're coming over. We want you to see our new car."

And they drove up in a bright red convertible.

"It looked so neat!"

It is not true that these kinds of people are not *thinking*. But "when they see the bright red convertible," the intellectual and analytic processes get preempted by the feeling and emotional responses. In another common scenario, these kinds of people make spontaneous judgments or decisions and then *rationalize* those responses with intellectual or analytic processes, after the fact. In general, the *thinking* portion of the population thinks and analyzes before it decides. The *feeling* portion makes spontaneous decisions, and then analyzes or rationalizes those decisions, after the fact.

These again are the adaptations: the *thinking*, cerebral, intellectual disciplined approach to matters and problems, versus the *feeling*, sensitive, responsive, emotional approach. (In Myers–Briggs terminology, we're talking about "Thinking" versus "Feeling.") The *balanced* approach is manifested by people who are able to draw equally well from both of these qualities.

These adaptations are sometimes referred to as "right brain" and "left brain." The "right brain" person is the artistic, sensitive, expressive kind of individual. The "left brain"person is the intellectual, analytical, disciplined individual, the one who is comfortable studying calculus, learning other languages, engaging in contemplative activities. Between them are "balanced" people who can call equally upon both their sensitive and their intellectual resources.

THREE STYLES

Cutting across these *adaptations* are three *styles*: the *polyactive* style, the *proactive* style, and the *reactive* style.

Polyactive individuals are people who have an innate or inherent capacity to deal with many different things at once. What's taking place here has to do NOT with left brain and right brain *differentiation*, but with left brain and right brain *communication*. It has to do with the facility with which we can draw on our various innate resources in order to deal with problems, with stress, with challenges, and so on. Polyactives are effective in dealing with different kinds of stress and different kinds of challenges and different kinds of demand; and they are effective in juggling many demands at the same time.

■ One observer reports:

> I remember sitting in our Shanghai office a few years ago with my wife, talking to the manager, who was also responsible for a cadre of Chinese translators. There was a little cubbyhole in the wall above his typewriter, through which he could communicate with the three or four Chinese translators who were in the adjoining room. He would pass them messages that he received in Chinese, and they would pass the translated materials back to him. And my friend was sitting there, talking to my wife and me in English; talking to the translators, through the open cubbyhole, in Chinese; and all the while he was doing that, he was typing out his monthly report.

Now, that is a *polyactive* person!

Polyactive people not only have this gift for doing several things at once, but are also typically confident and complacent about their skills and abilities, and their capacity to *cope*. Their life experiences have generally been successful. They expect that other people will respond to their needs and their requests. They are not overly concerned about being accepted or being well liked. They are *self*-directed; it is *their* interests and goals that are important; and they have had a lot of success in getting other people to accept their needs and to respond to them. Because of this, they are "natural born leaders" or "movers." It is easy for them to influence others; and other people tend to respond to them.

Proactives see what *polyactive* people are doing, and they ask, "How can I do that?" The answer is, that they learn how to plan ahead. If you are an effective *proactive* individual, you become a lifelong Boy Scout; your motto is, "Be prepared." You go through life anticipating the many different kinds of things that can happen to you, and that you may be required to do, and you make plans. Continuously.

If you find yourself wondering how you can learn to be *polyactive*, you're probably experiencing one of the *proactive* styles of response. If you're living among the *reactive* styles, the feeling is, "There's just no hope!" or "Why bother?"

In his effort to be like the polyactive, the proactive will systematically cover the front of his refrigerator with lists (or, in the computer world, he keeps his lists in the computer). If you're an inveterate list maker, you are probably living a proactive style, and you are trying to program yourself to anticipate things and to prepare for them. (Consider the young executive in California, who drives around with snow chains in the trunk of his BMW, because he never knows when he may have to go up to Arrowhead for a meeting.)

Polyactives don't have to plan ahead because they are *able* to take things as they come; and their life experience has been sufficiently successful so that they are confident that they can do that. They are very comfortable with a style that copes with life, as it happens. They may not always be tranquil; but they are not apprehensive. They come across as practical, pragmatic, realistic.

In contrast, *proactives* tend to be more optimistic, idealistic, reasonably confident (or at least cautiously confident) that they will be able to handle problems because they have *prepared* for them. Problems arise for these kinds of people when too many requirements descend upon them. No matter how big the refrigerator is, it can't take care of *everything*.

Reactives ask, "Why bother?" They feel that the world is "hopelessly" prearranged, and therefore it doesn't make any difference how you plan what to do. The government or taxes or the guy behind you with the eighteen-wheeler is going to preempt any constructive effort that you may put forward in any effort to try to cope. Their hope is to get through life with a minimum of difficulty; they are not in the habit of anticipating and avoiding problems; they are quite disposed to confront problems and to fight back when they occur. On balance, they tend to be fatalistic. Many are often pessimistic, viewing the world with apprehension, hoping for the best but expecting that bad things are going to happen.

- Polyactives are complacent, confident, self-directed, "now"-oriented.
- Proactives are idealistic, optimistic, forward-looking.
- Reactives are responsive, fatalistic, often pessimist. (See Figure 8.5)

Figure 8.5

Core Adjustments: #2			
Adaptations → **Styles** ↓	Right <u>Interactive</u> Emotional Expressive Spontaneous Feeling	Balanced <u>Organizational</u> Determined Committed Entrepreneurial	Left <u>Individualistic</u> Intellectualizing Deliberate Insulated Detached
Outer-Directed idealistic, dedicated mission-oriented conscientious planners; givers build for future "be prepared" can panic if overextended	Supporter	Idealist	Independent
Inner-Directed self-focused independent individualistic self-serving complacent live now/takers "project" stress	Performer	Organizer	Leader/Aide

Outer-Directed
 (Controlled)
 controlling/need
   for control
 overwhelmed
 passive (inhibiting)
 can be precipitous
   or immobilized by
   pressure or stress
	Follower	Controller	Rule Keeper

REVIEWING ADAPTATIONS AND STYLES: HOW THEY AFFECT RESPONSES AND DECISION–MAKING

Those with a *thinking* or *left brain* adaptation tend to be individualistic, self–determining, and in charge of plotting their own way through life. They are intellectualizing, deliberate, and relatively insulated from others. They are relatively aloof, so that when the decisions they have to make come into conflict with the needs of others who are dependent upon them, they will make their deliberations with detachment and insulation. Again: this doesn't mean that they are uniformly cold and unfeeling; but in their view, there is only so much room for feeling in decision–making. They perceive themselves as realistic, as pragmatic, as objective. They feel that in management, you have to cut the fabric to fit the pattern. You bite the bullet. Feelings are not dominant.

In contrast, the *feeling* or *right brain* individuals tend to be more interactive, more responsive to others, more dependent on others in some way or other, and to be more emotional, more expressive, and more spontaneous and feeling in their response. They are more inclined to take the needs of others into account when they are making their decisions.

The *"balanced,"* organizational kinds of people represent a blend of these two. (They are likely to come out with "x's" in some of the Myers–Briggs scales.) They can draw upon both sides, or from all four quadrants of the array. They are less likely to see matters in an "either–or" sense. They view most problems from a broad perspective, and are more capable of weighing both personal and impersonal factors, to make rational, considerate, dispassionate decisions.

As managers, thinking, left–brain people are likely to be seen as objective, tough, and sometimes cold and unfeeling. Feeling, right brain people are likely to be seen as emotional, soft, and often indecisive. Balanced managers are likely to be seen as cool but usually considerate and fair.

Stylistically, polyactive people respond to what some psychologists call "an inner locus of control." What's important to them, is what's important to *them*. Their own needs, their own interests, their own goals, motivations, and expectations are the things that govern their response to affairs. They are self–focused, independent, individualistic, and relatively self-serving; and they are complacent or confident in their ability to handle events. They are confident of their coping skills, which have served them well. They are comfortable taking responsibility for managing events, and skillful in making others feel responsible for creating problems. If you are dealing with an individual who has a way of making *you* feel responsible for everything that goes wrong in the organization, or in your relationship—and especially if he succeeds in making you feel responsible for *his* own mistakes—then the chances are that you are dealing with a polyactive individual.

- If you come home and find out that dinner is burned, and your wife says, "If you'd get home on time, dinner would be ready for you." The implication is that it's *your fault* that the dinner is burned—and, if you find yourself feeling that it *is* your fault, then you are probably contending with a polyactive. This capacity to project problems onto others is a characteristic of the polyactive style of behavior. They are inner-directed; it's *their* needs that essentially determine the maps that they pursue through life. One way to deal with problems is to dump them on other people. It follows that polyactives are most comfortable being delegators.

The two other kinds of people—proactives and reactives—tend to be *outer*-directed. The things that drive them, the things that motivate them, the things they respond to tend to come from the outside world. These forces come from other people, job requirements, rules and regulations, cultural experience, and other sources *outside* themselves.

To *polyactives*, the world is something to be lived in to *their own* satisfaction; it's something to be used, as necessary or desirable, to suit their needs. To *proactives* and *reactives*, the world is an *imposing* environment. It's something you have to respond to, it's something you have to yield to in some way or another. So in that sense, both of these groups are *outer-directed*.

In being outer-directed and responsive to the stimulations that come from the outside world, *proactives* tend to regard the world's intrusion as *challenging*, as providing opportunity, as something to respond to, and as something to prepare for.

In contrast, the *reactives* tend to regard the world as a ruling and *confining* force. The world *controls* them, and it is often threatening or frightening. To some of them, it is a force which, in turn, has to be controlled. Otherwise it will "gobble you up." So rules, regulations, order, and discipline become the guidelines and the hallmarks for reactives. Most of them live in an orderly world. Most are comfortable following the rules they have learned, as long as they prove effective. They *create* order or they *impose* order. In a few cases, when their system fails, they react *against* order, by adopting an antisocial or rebellious role. These are rule-conscious individuals who either *conform* to rules or *invent and impose* rules or *rebel against* rules. Except for those among them who are capable of composing the rules and the regulations, they tend to be fatalistic. They feel the world is so full of rules, regulations, and forms from the IRS that there is nothing that you can do about it.

Polyactives are very comfortable living in the "here and now." They are now-oriented. They can enjoy what is going on right now, and they don't have to worry about tomorrow because that's another day, and they'll take care of that when it comes. So they can play hard, live hard, drink long into the night, and enjoy all of these feel-good kind of things; and they'll deal with tomorrow when it comes. They are comfortable making decisions as they come along.

Proactives have difficulty enjoying today because they are so preoccupied preparing for what is going to come. You can't go to the ball game today, because today's a school day, and there is school again tomorrow, and you have to be prepared for that. So they prepare. Insofar as decisions are foreseeable, they will "do *their* homework"; and since it is their homework, they are most comfortable working alone. As managers, they would often like to delegate to others, but they are likely to feel that "if you want something done right, do it yourself."

Reactives, by and large, are unable to enjoy what's going on today and see little sense in preparing for tomorrow. They spend a great deal of their time wishing that things had been better in the past and trying to figure out how they can possibly do anything about it but feeling that there's nothing that they really can do. So they either follow the rules or create a revolution in order to change the rules.

the rules. Their decision style can range from overcautious and overconcerned, to precipitous. As managers, they have difficulty delegating responsibility, except perhaps to others who are orderly and conforming like themselves.

■ One observer notes that anytime there is a flood, you'll see the three different styles portrayed on the 7:00 o'clock news. They'll take you down to Texas or Oklahoma or wherever it is, and they'll fly over the flood area in a helicopter. And the first thing you'll see are all the proactive folks who are up on the high ground with their campers or their tents, with the dog and with the kids. And they're cooking dinner on their propane stoves. They heard that the flood was coming and had the camper loaded with supplies left over from the Gulf War, and with planning and forethought they have fled to the safety of the high ground.

Then you go swooping down the river, and you see all the polyactives out there in their boats and canoes, and they're helping folks, pulling dogs out of the water, recovering TV sets and refrigerators, and so on. They are coping with it. They are making the best of it. They are dealing with what's going on, and they are not overwhelmed by it.

And finally, the last thing we see are two of the reactives— Mom and Pop on the roof of the house—floating downstream. Now, they got the same information as everyone else, but they've said, in effect, "It won't happen to us," or, "If it happens, it happens. There isn't anything you can do about it. When the flood hits, you make for the roof, and you wait for the helicopters."

In general, most of us display a reasonable degree of flexibility in the way in which we address our needs, meet the needs of others, and so on. Few of us live in a constant state of stress, coping with an endless array of oppressive problems.

In assessing managers, however, the focus is most often on how people will respond to *significant* problems, to stress situations, to challenging economic problems. And when we are addressing *these* kinds of problems, then it is useful to "sort the cards" in order to address the priorities that will enter into any particular manager's decision-making process. We want to say that "on a scale of 1 to 10, what comes first, what comes next."

Most of us exhibit a fair amount of flexibility in making "ordinary decisions." But when the crunch comes, the model is going to help us solve the question of how the individual will make *significant* decisions: whether he takes losses in order to keep people on board (because people and social concerns are more important to him than more abstract and "practical" matters); or whether he gets rid of people, because of qualities of independence, detachment, dedication to the *organization*, and so on.

When it comes to evaluating decision processes in relatively critical circumstances, it is useful to know some things about people.

Left brain and polyactive people tend to view life and its programs and their activities in an individualistic way. They ask, "How is it this of significance to what *I* am trying to do? What can *I* do? What kinds of actions and activities can *I* effect?"

Right brain and proactive individuals tend to be more interactive, and to be dependent on others either as a source of guidance or as source of stimulation, encouragement, and response.

Balanced individuals tend to be organizational or institutional in their orientation. In other words, it's *entities* that are important. We have three fundamentally different kinds of decision responders:

-- *I* am important;
-- *People* are important;
-- *Organizations*, or *entities*, are important.

INTERACTIVE DYNAMICS

The Adaptations

The Balanced/Organizational Adaptation

Organizations are important for all the members of the *balanced* adaptations (Figure 8.6). What differentiates the proactive *idealist* from the polyactive *organizer* and the reactive *controller*? All three of these individuals are interested in the organizations, the environments, or the cultural group, or the ethnic group, or the street gangs from which they come or of which they are a part. How are they *different*? How can we tell them apart? What difference does it make, in corporate style or managerial decision-making?

Figure 8.6

Balanced: #2

	Idealist	
	Organizer	
	Controller	

The polyactive *organizers* (or *entrepreneurs*) see their organizations as an extension of themselves. And the prototypic entrepreneurial leader feels that "the organization is the reflection of *me*. What's good for the organization is good for *me*; what's good for *me* is good for the organization." The focus is on making them "better," bigger, more productive, and more prosperous. And there is a pragmatic, realistic, and (very often) a materialistic tenor to the effort. It is in their nature to be challenging, energetic, and hard-driving.

Proactive *idealists* (or *conservators*) are also organizational in their focus. Their interest is also in making the organization, the institution, the church, the party, the neighborhood, or whatever it is that defines them, "better"; but there is a recognizably strong element of *idealism* and *value* in their commitment. Their goal in life is to preserve the beliefs and codes that are important to them, and to make the world safe for these values and goals. So the *establishmentarian*, so to speak, lives here. His operating style is to be optimistic and encouraging, to perpetuate "good things" and "good purposes."

The reactive *controller* is also interested in the organization; but his interest tends to *dominate* it, to regulate it, to force conformity on it. He takes charge of an organization, in order to effect *control*. With his often suspicious, fatalistic, and pessimistic outlook, he fears that without his personal and intense supervision there will be chaos. There are few others he can trust to keep things in order. The best way to avoid mistakes is to not allow anybody to do anything. It may not be his purpose to inhibit the organization, but that is the ultimate effect. His management style tends to discourage imagination, initiative, risk, and growth.

- The recent fate of the Eastern Airlines Shuttle is of interest in these differentiations. At the center, there was the contest between Donald Trump and Frank Lorenzo for domination of that beleaguered carrier. During the "preliminaries," an Eastern Shuttle flight attendant was asked what would happen if Donald Trump took over. She said that she and her colleagues were looking forward to his takeover. When she was asked, "Wouldn't it be nice, for once, if Eastern Airlines had somebody at the top who knew something about running an airline?" She had a response ready. "We don't have any problem with Mr. Trump in that regard," she explained. "We know, from his past record, that when he takes over, he will appoint someone who knows about the airline business to run the show." And that was the perception on the part of the airline personnel, when they voted with their feet and their careers, to support Trump rather than Lorenzo. They had lived with Lorenzo, whose management style was controlling and strangling Eastern out of existence (as it had with People's Express and Texas Air and Continental). And they opted for (the more polyactive) Trump and threw their support to him. From *his* record, they felt he would make the organization *better*, by delegating its operation to a competent manager.

You have to be *self*-confident in order to delegate to others. If you have confidence in yourself, you have the confidence to delegate responsibility to others, leaving yourself free to chase after other opportunities (and to take back control from those managers who prove unfit for their tasks). This is the style of the *organizer*, or *entrepreneur* in this model.

If you don't have confidence in yourself, you can't have confidence in others. You don't trust others to take actions, for fear that they will make mistakes. You manage by *controlling*, inhibiting, precluding, and preempting action; and you strangle your lieutenants and the organization in the process. And that is the style of the *controller* in this model.

The Thinking, Left Brain Adaptation

The *independent*, the *leader/aide*, and the *rule keeper* are all self–oriented, independent, thinking, analytic, aloof, or detached in their manner (Figure 8.7). How can we differentiate among them? How do they differ in their corporate or managerial behavior?

Figure 8.7

Left Brain

		Independent
		Leader/Aide
		Rule Keeper

Proactive *independent* people tend to be *technocrats* or *intellectuals*. Scientists, technicians, artisans, and specialists of various kinds (including dedicated hobbyists) are likely to be found within this adaptation. Where values and goals are of particular moment to the *idealists*, and the organization is of central concern to the *organizers*, the *independents* tend to be motivated by ideas concepts, or activities that are uniquely important *to them*. When they do reach out beyond themselves, it is within a "community of interest": they are most comfortable with other people who share the same interests or who cherish the same activities. Someone once observed that "the chiefs of police of Beijing and Atlanta have more in common than either has with his own mayor." He was making a comment about the orientation and perspectives of the *independents*. It follows that their sense of loyalty and commitment flows more to these shared ideas and activities than to the institutions or corporations of which they are a part. While they can be leaders "among their own kind," they are not likely to seek leadership or management responsibilities in a more general sense, or as an end in themselves. As managers, they are likely to be quite parochial— perhaps very good at managing what is of significance to them and "pushing their own interests," but not much concerned with "the larger perspective." Leaders of technical and professional organiz- ations, who lobby on behalf of their own professional interests, are likely to emerge from this adaptation. They're not likely to be concerned for "what's good for General Motors." Their concern would be for the interests and welfare of "automotive engineers," "free exchange among nuclear scientists," or the rights of motor- cyclists to ride without helmets.

Polyactive *leader/aides*, in contrast, *are* inherently interested in leadership and management. Taking charge, or advising and influencing those who are in charge, is the stuff that turns them on. They seek responsibility, power, authority, and prestige; and there is an element in their commitment that is particularly personal and self–centered. They have a transient quality. They can take their leadership or influence from one organization to another, or from one mentor to another. While they are committed and loyal "wherever they are," they are able to take the commitment with them. Their ultimate loyalty is to themselves. Hence a John Sculley can be just as dedicated to Apple as to Pepsi. And Ed Rollins can advise George Bush one day and Ross Perot the next, with equal dedication and detachment.

Reactive *rule keepers* are less interested in leading (or advising) than in "keeping track," maintaining order, or insuring compliance. They are the accountants and umpires and police of the world, not necessarily making rules but making sure that others follow them. It is a lifestyle as much to be found in the schoolroom, the bedroom, or the kitchen, as in the boardroom or the precinct. Rule keepers are most comfortable working alone, or as specialists within a well-regulated group (combat patrols, SWAT teams, brokerage firms, church committees, neighborhood councils). They are not likely to *seek* leadership. If they are required to be managers, they are likely to be most effective managing highly structured organizations and activities, where they can enforce "good rules" that they have learned well. Otherwise, they are likely to be unimaginative, narrowly focused, and preoccupied with detail.

The feeling, right brain adaptations

The *supporters, performers,* and *followers* are all feeling, right brain people (Figure 8.8) As such, they reflect a kind of social dependency. They are aware of other people and sensitive to their relationships and interactions with them. In critical matters, relationships play an important role in their behavior. Their decision-making tends to be spontaneous. Often impulsive feelings and reactions will dominate their decisions; analysis, procedures, rules, and regulations will all be secondary.

Figure 8.8

Right Brain

Supporter		
Performer		
Follower		

Proactive *supporters* have a paternalistic attitude toward the world. They are the world's lifelong "co-dependents": they are here to nourish it, to protect it, to take care of it. As managers, they obviously want to make the workplace a pleasant and supportive environment. Yet, it is difficult for them to be objective and detached. They are at risk of being "overinvolved" with their personnel and caught up with social or interpersonal issues that may not always be relevant to progress or to the organization's "best interests" (as viewed by stockholders or *Standard and Poor's*).

The inner-directed, polyactive *performers* are also vulnerable to "overinvolvement," but it is *their* fortunes and careers that they are concerned about—not their colleagues' or their employees'. There is a dramatic or theatrical quality to performers' lifestyle. They command, and demand, attention and recognition. For them, the world exists as an audience, to respond to their needs and presence, to applaud them or otherwise to reward them. *Supporters* are "at risk" of being self-sacrificing at critical times. *Performers* are more likely to be self-indulgent (or, at least, self-concerned). When the chips are down, their decisions are likely to reflect *their* best interests, even at the expense of their colleagues or the organization as a whole.

To reactive *followers* the world exists to tell them what to do, either through leaders, institutional routines, or well-defined creeds. They can be loyal, dedicated, and committed, even self-sacrificing, but they need a structure to work within. Without it, they lack initiative and self-direction. In the corporate environment, they are most at risk of being promoted "above their level of incompetence," where they can find themselves surviving on past laurels and groping to define institutional goals and purposes. As managers, they are likely to be uncertain and indecisive or, at times, impulsive and precipitous.

The Styles

The Proactives

The supporters, idealists, and independents are all proactive in their response style (Figure 8.9). Accordingly, they are all forward-looking, outer-directed, and responsive in some way to a world outside themselves. They find that world to be challenging and provocative, something they want to be involved in. They want to protect it, or support it, or improve upon it in some positive way (at least, from their point of view). They tend to be concerned for the future, usually in an optimistic (if sometimes cautious) way.

The feeling, right-brain *supportive* people are in the world to take care of others, to nourish, to nurture. By way of illustration, consider a woman whose succession of careers (besides wife and

Figure 8.9

Proactive		

Supporter	Idealist	Independent

mother) are nurse, librarian, church secretary, and now, travel agent. What are the common qualities and characteristics that run through all these positions? They are all service–oriented activities; she moves from rendering one kind of service, to rendering another kind of service. That's what "turns her on." And, in return for the service that *they* render, these supportive people expect to get recognition, appreciation, and reward. They are hard–working and sacrific– ing individuals, but we have to recognize their sacrifice and let them know that we appreciate it. If we fail to do so, they can get distressed and antagonistic because we do not appreciate them. We noted earlier that these *supporters* are at risk of being overinvolved as managers. Given that it is "lonely at the top," they may find themselves so isolated, as managers, that they can't get the appre– ciation and support that is essential to sustain them. This can cause them to be uncertain and indecisive.

The balanced *idealists*, or *conservators*, are strongly identified with their origins, whatever those happen to be. (We can have Arab idealists and Israeli idealists beating each other over the head, while both of them are tying to make the world better for both.) It's their origins and their goals that they identify with. We can anticipate that as managers, *idealists* will seek solutions that best fulfill the ideal purposes and long–term goals of the organization—sometimes at the expense, if necessary, of short–term profit or personnel considerations.

The left brain, disciplined, and analytic *independent* intellectuals and technocrats are champions of the *ideas* or *activities* that are important to them, and they pursue a course in life that makes it possible for them to do what they want to do and to make those things better and to share with others who cherish the same interests—whether it's constructing theoretical models, building dams and bridges, playing chess, or racing automobiles. As managers, the critical decisions for them are those that affect the core interests, or ideas, of practices that are important to them.

■ A singular example is Werner Von Braun and his collection of rocket scientists. During World War II they developed rockets intended to destroy the British Isles. When the war ended, their special purpose ended. Unlike the vast majority of German intellectuals and professionals who stayed in Germany to rebuild the country and to make Germany better after the war, these people sought another place where they could continue to build rockets. It was a toss up, whether they were going to build rockets for us or build rockets for the Russians. We outbid the Russians, so they came and built rockets for us. The important thing for them was rocket engineering and space development, and they were willing to go wherever they needed to, in order to continue to work on those kinds of things.

It's also interesting, in this regard, to look at the personalities that were arrayed in San Diego, in the most recent pursuit of the America's Cup, and the different kinds of images presented by Dennis Conner and Paul Cayard.

■ Paul Cayard is the American yachtsman who was trying to win the America's Cup for the Italians. That is a marked contrast from the Dennis Conner image, four years earlier.

Conner was ready to take on the whole world, in order to get the America's Cup back to where the America's Cup *belongs* (in his sense of the proper order of things). For Conner, there is a goal, an issue, a principle at stake.

Four years later we have another American yachtsman who is interested in *winning a race* for anyone who can give him the best boat. It's obvious that driving boats and winning races is what's important for Cayard, not who it is that you win the race for.

The Polyactives

Being *polyactive*, the *performers*, the *organizers*, and the *leader/aides* are all inner-directed, self-sufficient, confident, and comfortable with living in the here and now (Figure 8.10). How are they differentiated in terms of managerial performance and decision-making?

Figure 8.10

Polyactive		
Performer	Organizer	Leader/Aide

Those who are labeled *performers* view the world as something to be lived in, dealt with, exploited (in the sense that life's a bowl of cherries and you scarf up as many as you can). The rest of the world exists to respond to them and their needs, and to applaud or at least to acknowledge their existence and importance. Because of these qualities, they are also called *theatrical* or *dramatic*. It doesn't follow that everyone in the theater lives here, or do all theatrical personalities seek careers on the stage. But a lot of theatrical *personalities* do live here; and all theatrical personalities project a sense of drama. We characterize these people as *theatrical* in the sense that they live their lives in a public and highly expressive way, making an issue of their presence, seeking attention and adulation. In a sense, they "take up more space" than the rest of us. You become very aware of their presence.

With people like Elizabeth Taylor, Marion Barry, or Charles de Gaulle it's not so much the role they perform as their *presence* that commands (and demands) attention and response. These are the people whose lifestyles compel attention. What's important to them is the recognition, the response from the rest of the world that assures them that they are in some way important. "You don't have to love me, but don't ignore me!" As managers or social or political leaders, their behavior inescapably brings attention to themselves more than to their deeds or their achievements *per se*. Ronald Reagan once noted, "It's remarkable how much you can accomplish, if you don't care who gets the credit." He was NOT talking about the dramatic, theatrical, performer personality. They DO care that THEY get the credit, the attention, and the recognition for whatever they do. And whatever *they* do is okay, because *they* do it.

Those whom we call *organizers* (often seen as entrepreneurs) are trying in their inner-directed way to make their organizations bigger, better, more powerful, more significant. A bewildered public may reasonably ask, "Why does Donald Trump (or Robert Maxwell or Jack Kent Cooke) keep acquiring more and more real estate, airlines, money? Doesn't he have enough?" And for these entrepreneurs, this question has no meaning. It's not a question of "*enough*". It's the growth, the expansion, the continuing achievement, the ego enhancement, that is important. They are *not* seeking a *finite* goal; they are pursuing endless enlargement. They perceive themselves as inherent to the organization. There is an intense interaction between the two, a sense of identity, of projection, of symbiosis between the individual and his organizational ego. Charlie Wilson observed that "What's good for General Motors is good for the USA." As managers, organizers feel that "What's good for the organization is good for *me!*"

Their management goals reflect this compulsion for continuous advancement and growth. They have the confidence to take risk, to delegate responsibility to others (and to get rid of them if they fail). Delegating matters to others leaves them free to pursue other opportunities for growth and fulfillment. To live is to grow. Stop growing, you die.

Leader–aides are similar in many respects to organizers: they tend to take command, to rise to the top, and to run things; or they seek to exercise influence over those who do. As opposed to the organizer–entrepreneur (whose focus tends to be on the organization, as his "larger ego"), the focus of the *leader–aide* is on *himself*.

This *self*–orientation of the *leader*, versus the *balanced* orientation of the *organizer–entrepreneur*, can be observed in the images that were presented to us by the military commanders in Desert Storm, versus the military commanders who led our forces in World War II. The World War II military commanders tended to be of the *leader–nature*, while the Desert Storm military commanders presented themselves as being of the balanced, organization–identified type. MacArthur said, "I have returned!" Colin Powell and Norman Schwartzkopf were more likely to say, "*We* are going to achieve." There was a uniquely new manifestation of concern for the welfare of the troops, with a strong implication that strategies and tactics were being planned with troop losses very much in mind. This is a vast departure from the leadership images that were projected in Vietnam, World War II, and certainly in the earlier World War and before.

The Reactives

While *polyactives* tend to dominate the world, and *proactives* feel challenged to support it or improve upon it, *reactives* view the world as an imposing and often threatening environment (Figure 8.11). They feel compelled to obey it, fight it, or keep it from getting out of control. The *followers*, the *controllers*, and the *rule keepers* present three different ways of responding to this hostile environment.

The *followers* need direction and discipline in order to function effectively. Left to their own resources, they don't know what to do. We might call these the "enlisted men" of the world. It doesn't mean that all the military's enlisted troops live here; it does mean that these kinds of people thrive best in an organized or institutional kind of environment, where leaders or procedures tell them what to do. They are the followers, the doers, the worker–bees of the world, largely unconcerned about goals and purposes and ideals. Insofar as they follow orders, they feel they should otherwise be left alone. Such people are *not* likely to *seek* positions of leadership. If managerial responsibilities are thrust upon them, they are immensely dependent on supportive aides. Lacking good staff, they are likely to be very inhibited, uncertain about their goals, and indecisive.

Controllers live in fear of chaos. They abhor the prospect of organizations running "out of control," and they do not have the confidence to entrust authority and responsibility except to others who are "orderly." As managers, they use their positions of authority to *impose* control, establishing elaborate codes of rules and regulations and micromanaging everything within their purview. They shrink from innovation and risk-taking.

Figure 8.11

Reactive

Follower	Controller	Rule Keeper

In the corporate world, *rule keepers* are the happy minions of the controllers. Their mission in life is to keep everything orderly, and to keep others "on track," carefully coloring within the lines. Left to their own resources, they are more likely to be found in the accounting and other administrative offices and task forces, than in the boardrooms and the executive suites. Within the parameters of these regulatory activities, they can be very effective specialists and very conscientious (if narrow and compulsive) team members. If they move into the management ranks, it is likely to be at the top of their chosen specialties—as chiefs of some highly organized and well-defined activity. If they are elevated to responsibilities of a more general nature, their style is likely to be inhibiting, controlling, and risk-averse. They are not likely to favor innovation; they will pay more attention to the "bottom line" than to the subtleties or niceties of personnel management. Table 8.1 summarizes the interplay of these dynamics.

Table 8.1

Dynamics Table

	SUPPORTER	IDEALIST	INDEPENDENT
General Style	Supportive	Idealistic	Dedicated, committed
Focus	Other people	Core values, goals	Parochial: "Community of interest"
Priorities	People, service	Preserve values, improve institutions	"Push" special goals
Management Style	Supportive, "happy ship"	Supportive, encouraging, calculated risk	Aggressive, narrow
Vulnerability	Overinvolvement	Disillusionment	Narrow perspective

	PERFORMER	ORGANIZER	LEADER/AIDE
General Style	Dramatic, self-promoting	Optimistic, challenging	Aggressive, dominating
Focus	Own needs, recognition	Organization, resources, personnel	Leadership, influence, advancement
Priorities	Personal acclaim	Growth	Take charge, exert influence
Management Style	Press own interests	Encourage, challenge, delegate; "fair"	Aggressive, self-confident
Vulnerability	Ignore broad obligations	Overextend resources Underassess risks	Exceed mission Overreach

Table 8.1 cont'd

Dynamics Table

	FOLLOWER	CONTROLLER	RULE KEEPER
General Style	Get along	Fearful, mistrustful	Controlling, enforcing
Focus	Do the job	Maintain control	Procedures, rules
Priorities	Narrow	Avoid risk and chaos	Impose rules
Management Style	Limited vision, indecisive	Controlling, inhibiting	Petty, narrow
Vulnerability	Immobilized, miss opportunity	Strangle innovation, impede growth	Inhibit creativity, ignore broader needs

Each of the nine core categories is portrayed with respect to its "general style" of behavior or orientation, the "focus" of its attention; the "priorities" with which it addresses major problems or decisions; its "management style," which characterizes the foundation or the basis from which it makes management decisions; and its "vulnerabilities," in terms of the risks, the shortcomings, or the potential areas of failure that are likely to derive from this pattern of management or leadership.

OBSERVING AND INFERRING:
THE GLOBAL DIMENSIONS OF THE MODEL
Figure 8.12 suggests how all of this "comes together": how the forces and dynamics that have been presented so far enable us to make sense out of what we observe or what we otherwise learn about people (and organizations); and how this in turn gives us some sense of how that person is likely to think or respond in significant circumstances.

We start at the center of this array, with a (clearly) hypothetical person who is an eminently capable organizer, able to draw on all available resources and coping skills, Such a person would be able to maintain independence of judgment, while addressing the needs of others and profits from the information they can provide. He would be feeling and sensitive, but emotionally controlled. He would deal effectively with today's problems, enlightened by errors of the past, while preparing effectively for the future. He would be positive in outlook, challenged by opportunity, undaunted by obstacles He would be confident of his own abilities, comfortable with others, practical and realistic in his judgments.

Figure 8.12

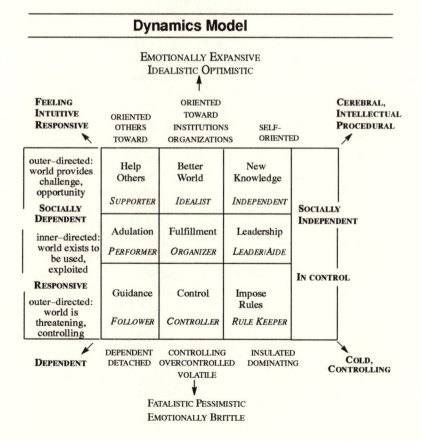

Dynamics Model

EMOTIONALLY EXPANSIVE
IDEALISTIC OPTIMISTIC

FEELING INTUITIVE RESPONSIVE	ORIENTED TOWARD	ORIENTED TOWARD INSTITUTIONS ORGANIZATIONS	SELF-ORIENTED	CEREBRAL, INTELLECTUAL PROCEDURAL
outer–directed: world provides challenge, opportunity **SOCIALLY DEPENDENT**	Help Others *SUPPORTER*	Better World *IDEALIST*	New Knowledge *INDEPENDENT*	**SOCIALLY INDEPENDENT**
inner–directed: world exists to be used, exploited **RESPONSIVE**	Adulation *PERFORMER*	Fulfillment *ORGANIZER*	Leadership *LEADER/AIDE*	**IN CONTROL**
outer–directed: world is threatening, controlling	Guidance *FOLLOWER*	Control *CONTROLLER*	Impose Rules *RULE KEEPER*	

DEPENDENT

DEPENDENT DETACHED	CONTROLLING OVERCONTROLLED VOLATILE	INSULATED DOMINATING	COLD, CONTROLLING

FATALISTIC PESSIMISTIC
EMOTIONALLY BRITTLE

He would also be extremely hard to find.

As we move from this central point, toward the top of the mode—toward "12 o'clock," so to speak—we encounter people who are less objective and pragmatic, but who are increasingly optimistic and idealistic in their attitudes and their expectations. These people have strong sense that the world is inherently good, that it can be even better, and that they can contribute toward that improvement.

As we move in the opposite direction, toward the bottom of the mode, toward 6 o'clock, optimism gives way to fatalism and pessimism, a sense that the world is demanding and confining. There is a morbid feeling that the world is at risk of spinning out of control, that at best it needs to be harnessed and at worst there is nothing you can do about it. Order must be defined and imposed; rules must be issued and obeyed. One's choices in life are to confirm, or to rebel.

As we move to the right of the chart—toward 3 o'clock—we encounter independence and self-sufficiency. "Other people" become less important than ideas or procedures of personal achievement.

As we move toward the left side of the chart, toward 9'clock, we observe people who are more and more dependent on others. They need relationships with others to provide them with guidance and direction, to give life meaning and purpose, or to give proof of their importance.

Toward the upper right, toward 1:30, we find people who are strongly devoted to their own ideas and interests: the intellectuals, the dedicated technicians, the people with a strong commitment to their chosen activities or processes. The farther we go along this axis, the narrower the focus and the more intense the commitment.

In the opposite direction, toward 7:30, we find people who are increasingly dependent on guidance and direction. Without leaders or institutions to guide them (or when their is no one around to tell them what to do), they are aimless. At best, they have "nothing to do"; on the negative side, they become vulnerable to adventitious or transient influence that can often provide them with "bad leadership." This is one of the potential sources for all the idle hands that can serve the Devil.

As we move toward the upper lift, toward 10:30, we encounter people who are increasingly sensitive and involving, people whose interests are directed toward other persons and toward social issues that have an emotional or empathic context.

Moving in the opposite direction, toward 4:30, the social atmosphere becomes increasingly cold, detached, and emotionally distant. At the extremes, these are the people who can range from coldly ruthless to deliberately cruel, in "laying down the law" to anyone within their reach.

The salience of this dynamics model is that most of us are inherently consistent in our attitudes and behavior. While we are reflect some range and degree of flexibility in responding to challenges and resolving problems, we all harbor a core of feelings experiences, needs, and motives that shape our approach to life's diverse demands. This being the case, the model informs us that relatively small amounts of information about a person can assist us in making reasonably effective judgments about how he will go about coping with significant problems. We do not *always* need large amounts of highly detailed information, assiduously analyzed by experts, to make reasonable judgments about where other people are coming from, or where they are going. A little information can often take us a long way.

WRAPPING UP

We noted at the outset that there are many times, in the competitive intelligence effort, when we are faced with questions that cannot be answered directly from observations alone, or from personal or corporate histories. They have to do with corporate leaders and key management personnel, and they bear on the decision-making process. What factors does he take into consideration in making key decisions? What are his priorities? Is he dedicated to the growth of his company, the welfare of his employees, or his own personal advancement? Is he willing to take significant risks? Can he "bet the farm?" And if he will, what will push him? Impulsivity? Careful homework? The advice of others? His own self-confidence? In the final analysis, what does he want? Corporate success? Personal glory? Unending growth? How will he respond to a significant challenge in the marketplace? With initiative? With caution? Hunkering down to avoid disaster?

The profiling model generates answers to these kinds of questions.

It enables us to locate an individual within the model, based on *observable* behavior and past performance; and the model provides the basis for answering the *unobservable* and *intangible* question. (See Figure 8.13.)

Figure 8.13

Inferential Profiling Model

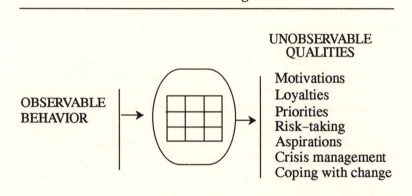

UNOBSERVABLE
QUALITIES

OBSERVABLE
BEHAVIOR

Motivations
Loyalties
Priorities
Risk–taking
Aspirations
Crisis management
Coping with change

We know, for example, that people with a methodical approach to their work and a history of planning ahead in realistic terms are most likely to be proactive. Persons with a great deal of self-confidence, who have *earned* the right to be complacent about their personal and managerial skills (based on a history of effective coping) are likely to be polyactive. The chronically suspicious and apprehensive person who has little confidence in others is likely to be reactive.

Those who are comfortable in making their own decisions and in taking responsibility for themselves and, when necessary, for others, are likely to be left brain. Those who are responsive to others because they want to help, because they need guidance, or because they have a great need for attention, are likely to be right brain–oriented, in model terms. Those who seem able to deal equally well (or, perversely, equally *badly*) with both these qualities, are likely to be "balanced"—able to take the needs of others into account, without getting overly involved (or, at the other end of the spectrum, unable to come to a decision when weighing "people needs" against " organizational needs").

Insofar as we can "line people up" in both dimensions, often on the basis of fairly limited amounts of information, we can make a reasonably accurate assumption of "where they live" within the model. These first efforts can guide our search for more information (to confirm our assessment); or they can give us some comfort in making our first judgments about our subject.

We know, for example, that polyactives will have considerable comfort in taking risk—especially in areas where they can evaluate the variables and exercise some control over them. They make good poker players: they can figure the odds, manipulate them with their own behavior (bluffing with great comfort, when necessary), and they are not afraid to lose. Proactives are masters of the "calculated risk," collecting all the relevant information, avoiding the potholes, betting cautiously on what they can evaluate as a "good prospect." They are comfortable looking at the "long haul" (and in their own portfolios, they are probably well invested in bonds and mutual funds). Reactives are more likely to be erratic, to have difficulty coming to a decision, to be overly inhibited (out of fear of failure), or to be impulsive (fatalistic, "taking a chance"). Lotteries probably thrive on the "faith" of reactives: they "know" there is nothing *they* can do to improve their fortunes, so they opt for sheer, unmanaged luck.

We know that the primary loyalty of the left brain adaptations is to themselves. They can be intensely loyal to their organizations, but they are wholly capable of carrying that loyalty to another organization if a transfer suits their own personal needs. The right brain adaptations have a greater investment in other people (although the theatrical performers can be very self-centered, seeking attention from others rather than reaching out to them for guidance or to support them). In return for their loyalty, they need guidance, support, and recognition; and they can transfer their commitment to others who are willing to provide the support or the attention that they need. In this sense, an organization is "safest" (i.e., stable, protected) in the hands of the idealist and the organizers, because of the strong sense of identity that they have with their institutions.

Polyactives need a sense of achievement. They need to feel that they are making progress for *themselves*. Proactives pursue a sense of accomplishment: they seek to fulfill *goals*, to "make things better" for the people who depend on them, for the institutions that are dear to them, or for the ideas or the activities that are important to them. Reactives are most likely to be comfortable "just doing things." Within an organization, meetings are a way in which polyactives "get things done"; they are a necessary evil for proactives; they can be an end in themselves for reactives.

Crisis management is what the proactive leader is continually planning for. It's a challenging and stimulating "ball game" for polyactives. It's the graveyard for reactives, who will still be looking for their weapons when the battle is over.

In short, the model provides the clues for answering many of the questions we are concerned with in our efforts to understand corporate managers. While there are many bewildering areas in corporate intelligence, understanding the leaders and managers among our clients and competitors does not have to be one of them. Conventional intelligence systems inform us about our competitors' resources, their patterns of investment, and their past success as performers. Taken together, they can inform us of what our competitors *can* do, what they *might do*. But taken alone, they do not tell us what they are *likely* to do or what they *will* do, especially in making critical decisions while under critical pressure.

Profiling gives us clues in these vital areas. It provides the added dimension, the added value that can make our competitive intelligence efforts truly effective.

ACKNOWLEDGMENTS

I have created this model as an original presentation which draws conceptually from the published and unpublished works of Dr. John W. Gittinger and Dr. David R. Saunders.

Gittinger's *Personality Assessment System* is a psychometrically based clinical model. It postulates inherent predispositions of an intellectual, temperamental, and social nature, and traces their development as they are molded and shaped by interactions with the social or cultural environment. The PAS model uses observable behavior or psychological test data to determine the trajectory of individual development and to anticipate its continuing development and, therefore, its responses to new life experiences.

Saunders' *Reference Group Model* is a meticulous mathematical model that evolves from and supplements Gittinger's PAS. It emerges from a systematic examination of thousands of clinical cases, from which it classifies and categorizes people on the basis of shared psychometric and behavioral characteristics.

These two related models are, collectively, expansive enough to address all forms of human behavior, in its enormous complexity. The model presented here represents an enormous simplification and generalization of the parameters and concepts that are addressed by Gittinger and Saunders. While this presentation could not exist without the resources provided by these two latent models, all the shortcomings and limitations inherent in *this* application are the exclusive responsibility of this author.

Marshall N. Heyman

REFERENCES

Heyman, Marshall N. "A Brief Explanation of the Personality Assessment System." *Personality Assessment System Journal*, vol. 1, no. 1, Spring 1982, 7–10.

Krauskopf, Charles J., and David R. Saunders. *Personality and Ability: The Personality Assessment System.* Lanham: University Press of America (in preparation).

Matarazzo, J. D. 1972. *Wechsler's Measurement and Appraisal of Adult Intelligence.* 5th ed. Baltimore: Waverly Press.

Saunders, David R. "Fundamental Facts about Reference Groups." *Personality Assessment System Foundation Journal*, vol. 5, 1989, 5–38.

Winne, John F., and John W. Gittinger. "An Introduction to the Personality Assessment System." *Journal of Clinical Psychology.* Monograph Supplement #38, April 1973, 3–67.

Chapter 9

The Triad of Business, Government, and Academe

Each year, companies and governments make thousands of decisions.... There are new rules behind those decisions, new rules for global business success.[1]

Two decades ago, Airbus Industrie began to build and market commercial jet liners. A consortium of four different European government-led R&D investment and multinational pooling of supply and manufacturing expertise has moved Airbus from 0 percent market share just over twenty years ago to about 30 percent share today. Airbus is now a very competitive player in the commercial aircraft market. Twenty years ago, Boeing and McDonnell Douglas did not take this new European consortium very seriously. In Asia, Japanese government agencies and businesses, the Ministry of International Trade and Industry, the Japanese External Trade Organization, Japanese banks, advertising agencies, and major industries have been working together for a long time and with well-known results. There was a delayed U.S. recognition of the competitive threats posed by these new initiatives. Examples of these "new" rules of the game are now legion. Partnerships, even between or among competitors such as the International Aero Engine Consortium, are a primary characteristic of these new rules. In fact, however, these are *not* new rules. These are relatively old rules and they are someone else's rules, not ours. Our competitors are playing the game of business, including the competitive intelligence game, by their rules. One of the rules, old to them but new to us, is linkage between the public and private sectors. The point: if we are to be competitive in global markets, we must adopt and adapt to these concepts, these old rules, and make them our "new" rules of the intelligence industry, even though they may not have been invented here.[2]

The focus of this chapter is to suggest a model for adapting these old rules of partnerships and alliances and to develop our own new rules. We need to adopt new ways of thinking about how the intelligence industry can be linked or "partnered" to serve two pressing intelligence requirements: (1) building visibility, capability, and credibility for corporate intelligence programs, and (2) improving our business competitiveness in the changing global business environment by strengthening the fundamental source of competitiveness, intelligence. The triad of intelligence resources constitutes the major players or stakeholders in the industry, business, government, and academe. Each can play related roles in providing U.S. businesses and business managers with value-added opportunities to level the competitive playing field. Figure 9.1 summarizes the purpose and content of this book. It proposes a model or plan to help overcome the obstacles that have thus far limited the use and application of a basic and powerful source of competitive advantage—formal competitive intelligence systems.

Intelligence and its potential to strengthen positions of competitive advantage can be relatively portrayed by *their* approach and *our* approach to formal intelligence efforts.

Our foreign competitors share information. The French, Israeli, and Japanese intelligence services share information with their national businesses that give them an edge.

Figure 9.1

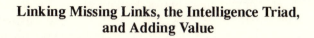

**Linking Missing Links, the Intelligence Triad,
and Adding Value**

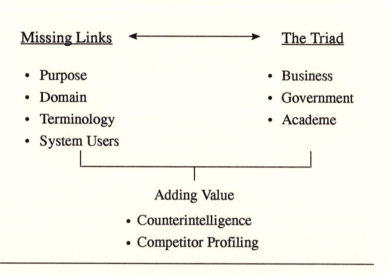

Missing Links ⟷ The Triad

- Purpose
- Domain
- Terminology
- System Users

- Business
- Government
- Academe

Adding Value

- Counterintelligence
- Competitor Profiling

We do not, as a matter of policy or practice, follow this rule.[3] The Central Intelligence Agency tracks and assesses a broad range of economic and technological information. Except in rare and narrowly focused areas that may relate to national security interests, the intelligence is not shared with the private sector. U.S. colleges and universities offer over one hundred courses for degree program students in the field of intelligence. Ninety-nine percent of these courses, though, are concerned with the traditional intelligence histories and issues of government and military intelligence. They reside in the political science, international studies, or history department curriculums, not in management.[4] Lund University, in Sweden, offers a major concentration in intelligence, with heavy emphasis on corporate intelligence in its economic and management program. The private sector and Swedish businesses, as well as the government, are intimately involved in the Lund program. Except in relatively generic and sanitized forms, those few U.S.

corporations having some history and experience with formal intelligence programs do not share their intelligence experiences with each other or with those two or three university–based corporate competitive intelligence programs. Further, while business and management students may benefit enormously by learning through the case method, there are, unfortunately, among the thousands of business and management cases, none that deal with the managerial problems, issues, and questions of formal intelligence programs.

How can we close this gap and move ahead

From	To

in order to come up to speed with our foreign competitors and improve our chances for profitability, growth, and survival? One answer is through sharing and partnering and linking the industry players and their special skills, experiences, and resources with intelligence learning and teaching and practice. What to learn should precede what to teach and how to teach.

THE LARGER ISSUE

Graduate schools of management and business have crafted an MBA-type curriculum consisting of required courses. These courses focus on pieces of the "international" theories of finance, trade, culture and so on, and functional activities such as manufacturing and marketing, with planning, policy, or ethics courses added as current fashion dictates. The curriculum reflects thinking on what should be taught as basics for what managers, leaders, or entrepreneurs should learn. The methodology of teaching varies for both "core" courses and the electives that may be offered in the hundreds of various programs. Further, the teaching and whatever learning may result from these programs are largely governed by whatever the faculty, deans, and administrators of the universities and their graduate business schools determine to be relevant. For years, there have been rumblings that U.S. management schools are not teaching the right things in the right ways. There is concern that what has been determined to be relevant is not very relevant in the real world of competition.

The point in making this observation is simply to suggest two things that are related to improving our corporate intelligence capabilities. First, training, educating and equipping intelligence providers is part of the larger process of training, educating, and equipping all managers to understand the complexities of managing any enterprise. Managers must plan, organize, act, and decide about purposes, goals, and actions, and *critically* think through the effects of these managerial activities in terms of risks, trade–offs, and options. Second, whatever it is that managers need to know or organize can be conveniently grouped under three headings.[5] They are:

◯	*Competitive Environment:*	forces external to the organization that can be influenced and perhaps partially controlled.
△	*Competitor Environment:*	competitors in the same external environment who can pose threats, opportunities, or new standards.
▢	*Internal Environment:*	our processes, operations, policies, which define culture or way of doing things, organizational and personal goals, and allocation of resources to support objectives.

These environments are linked as the total environment that defines the broad domain for management education, training, and knowledge. The provision, use, and management of the organization's intelligence resources are part of this broad domain. Not everything that could be an element of any of these three environments is necessarily applicable for all competitive intelligence programs. There are, however, some common factors and interests:

- understanding the appropriate domain and what defines the appropriate domain—the industry, competitors, and the organization.

- understanding the "intelligence market"—the customers and users—within the appropriate domain.

- defining a market and marketing plan that provides intelligence products and processes that are of intelligence value and use to users.

What intelligence providers need to know is both broad (i.e. the industry or competitive environment) and specific (i.e. the character- istics of the organizational environment). This general and specific requirement provides a real opportunity for the triad to team up and work together toward developing our intelligence resources into real sources of competitive advantage. No one player can undertake the challenging task of strengthening the intelligence advantage. The triad must work together as three legs supporting the intelligence efforts and programs.

THE BUSINESS LEG

In the game of business competition, the business is the intelligence command center. As a command center, the business organization can play two roles in strengthening its competitive intelligence resource and advantage.

Internal. Part of the intelligence provider's learning must take place within the organization. Only organization management can ultimately define the appropriate intelligence domain. Management must identify the external forces, including the industry character- istics and the organization's resource and market competitors, that are of significant interest and importance to the organization. To ensure that this defining requirement is met is an ongoing management responsi- bility for the intelligence staff. The relative importance of the elements in the "competitive environment," "competitor environment," and "organizational environment" will change over time. Intelligence provider and management training can be provided from internal sources, from outside businesses and industry consultants, and from government agencies such as the Department of Commerce and the Central Intelligence Agency. The Department of Commerce collects country, economic, and technological intelligence. The CIA can also provide learning experience in these areas as well as in appropriate areas of scenario planning, counterintelligence, and analysis that are specific to the needs of the organization.[6]

External. A general knowledge of and "intelligence" about the business environments are essential for business managers. Business organizations can assist university-based management and intelligence programs in providing this knowledge. Businesses can support relevant curriculum initiatives by providing speakers and visiting lecturers. It can assist with real intelligence case development and with suitable research opportunities. Hands-on project opportunities for students that provide for research, analysis, and critical thinking skill acquisition are also among the possibilities for linking business with academe, which has the general learning experience responsibility. Some random and isolated efforts at linkage are underway. The experience of these efforts can be refined, coordinated, and focused in a broader linkage of sharing and partnering.

THE GOVERNMENT LEG

If one key to a successful, effective formal intelligence program is in recognizing and utilizing all the appropriate industry sources of intelligence, experience, and expertise, then the untapped accumulations of government experience are valuable resources. Many government organizations collect economic, technological, demographic, and other forms of "competitive" information that become useful national intelligence. This competitive information could also be useful in the private sector.[7] While some government information is dated and not processed, other information is assessed in terms of forecasts, probabilities, and scenarios. Within the appropriate domain for the organizational intelligence provider, these available sources and resources should be identified and assessed. They are potentially new information and intelligence (and counterintelligence) assets that can be utilized by intelligence providers and users.

It is inefficient and often unproductive for intelligence providers to search for information and sources in government that may be useful. Rather than being reactive, government agencies can play a proactive role and take the initiative. This role includes training managers and intelligence staffs in areas where there is organizational need and corollary government experience and expertise. Analysis techniques, counterintelligence, personality profiling, scenarios, forecasting, and gaming are often common appropriate areas for both government and business intelligence systems. Government agencies, principally the Central Intelligence Agency, can help encourage the development of university-based intelligence courses and programs by providing speakers and teaching materials that are also common to government and corporate intelligence interests and needs. The CIA has a university outreach program that provides speakers and visiting lecturers to university-based government intelligence related courses and programs.[8] The government intelligence resources certainly exist, but they haven't been readily accessible to businesses or university management programs. They remain as hidden assets within highly structured, conventional, and functional organization boxes. The first step is a dialogue among the industry players to further explore needs, opportunities, and resources for furthering cooperative efforts.[9]

THE UNIVERSITY LEG

There are three things that universities and their graduate schools can do to strengthen the management learning experience.

First, they can redesign and focus their MBA-type programs on competitive advantage which, after all, is the implied (if not stated) purpose of many such programs. Information and its processed product of intelligence is the core management need and requirement. Revamping entire curriculums to meet some focused context and standard relating to intelligence is not in the realm of high probability. However, it is quite possible to take at least two steps in this general direction. More MBA programs could offer management intelligence courses that would suggest, if not stress, the crucial role of intelligence in a universal competitive environment. Such courses could draw on appropriate experts from business and government. Ideally, a prototype management program could be developed, either within an existing MBA curriculum or as an entirely new model by a new entrant. The program would focus the curriculum on information and intelligence, and the use of these assets in decision-making.

Second, universities and graduate schools can work closely with the business community in three areas: intelligence speakers, research, and case development. Visiting lecturers can bring some real-world learning and experience to the classroom. The topics and issues to be addressed must be carefully thought out, defined, and marketed to the appropriate corporate manager or intelligence user or provider. Research in the field of corporate intelligence and formal intelligence program processes and practices are essentially nonexistent. Additionally, cases in the field are also nonexistent. Business school faculty and business managers can share the initiative for developing and providing case studies that will enhance the academic intelligence learning experience. Hands-on projects where students act as "consultants" to a particular business group, gathering competitor information and assessing its meaning, can also have significant learning value and can be incorporated into an intelligence course syllabus. In my experience with five or six companies that have participated with my competitive intelligence course students over the past ten years, the results have been mixed. There is some student excitement and even interest in undertaking secondary research and formulating an intelligence "product" for the business sponsor. However, the business or industry may be only of marginal interest. The information provided by the sponsor may be so sanitized as to be quite sterile. Limiting students to secondary research tends to minimize the real-world learning experience. Nonetheless, the project idea is another sharing-partnering possibility.

It is unlikely that any of the individual or collective players in the industry will begin to take steps to link the industry triad into a coherent, cooperative stakeholder effort.   There is, however, a fourth industry player that plays a unique role as an intelligence resource and participant in the industry. The Society of Competitive Intelligence Professionals could be the catalyst. For those readers unfamiliar with the society, SCIP includes among its 1,800 or so members representatives from business, government, and academe. Table 9.2 presents some information about the society's stated purposes and activities.

SCIP is in a position, through its programs, networks, membership, and interests, to serve as the catalyst for change.[10] It can provide the initiative for a new paradigm and thinking about corporate intelligence and formal intelligence programs. It could help level the playing field and develop for U.S. corporations a powerful source of competitive advantage. The society, if it decides to do so, can energize the process to provide the missing links and opportunities to add value. It can begin the process of coherently linking the intelligence triad of business, government, and academe.

Figure 9.2

The Society of Competitive Intelligence Professionals
Purpose and Programs

STATEMENT OF PURPOSE

The Society of Competitive Intelligence Professionals (SCIP) is a non-profit organization of individuals who evaluate competitors and competitive situations and associate to improve their skills. The objectives of SCIP are to:

- Establish and promote competitive intelligence as a profession.

- Provide for the professional development of its members.

- Advocate high ethical standards for the profession.

- Advance the interests of the membership.

In just a few short years, SCIP has evolved to the point where we are the leading international association devoted to the field of competitive intelligence.

We need to constantly improve our existing services and products and create new ones.

Figure 9.2 cont'd

CHAPTERS

As part of the strategic plan developed over the past year, SCIP has made a commitment to grassroots development. The chief component of this grassroots movement is the development of City and Area Chapters. These have been established to meet the growing diversification of our membership both from an industry and geographic standpoint.

Chapters will continue to be established in areas where the number of members and interest warrant. They will enable professionals with common backgrounds and interests in competitive and business intelligence to network.

Source: Adapted from the Membership Directory, 1992, Society of Competitive Intelligence Professionals.

The purpose of this book has been to explore and discuss ways to improve U.S. business position and performance by more effectively utilizing the resources and assets of a formal intelligence system for competitive advantage. We need to generate growth, purpose, and understanding for this new industry and to now focus on the market, the users of intelligence, rather than the providers of intelligence. It is time to leverage ten years of experience and to take advantage of this window of opportunity to shift from the supply to demand side, and to move beyond conventional wisdom.

NOTES

1. I. Magaziner and M. Patinkin, *The Silent War*, (Random House, 1989). This book is organized into three sections: competing with low-wage countries, competing with developed countries, and competing in future technologies. Each section contains "case" studies of two countries and one U.S. corporation. If intelligence providers wish to add to their learning and library, this book is a useful addition. The quotation appears on p. viii.

2. In her article, "Imitation Versus Innovation: Lessons to Be Learned from the Japanese," *Organizational Dynamics,* Winter 1993, M. K. Bolton argues that while imitators are often labeled as "counterfeits," "clones," and "knockoffs," imitation is a strategy today that is more often successful than innovation. Imitation is related to the "not invented here" syndrome, and thus can be a negative driver of an innovation strategy. The analogy to intelligence and the lack of a common effort thus far among the triad is worth considering.

3. See the *Wall Street Journal,* August 4, 1992, "Business Secrets," and the *Washington Post,* February 4, 1993, "Administration to Consider Giving Spy Data to Business," for discussion of present and potential CIA roles in helping American corporations compete with foreign rivals. While former CIA director Gates opposed sharing "secrets" with U.S. firms, the new director, James Woolsey, said in his Senate confirmation hearings that the administration would review this policy.

4. The National Intelligence Study Center in its 1992 publication, "Teaching Intelligence in the Mid–1990's; A Survey of College and University Courses on the Subject of Intelligence," identifies only one of the one hundred or so courses as part of a school of management curriculum and as a corporate intelligence course.

5. The three headings correspond to the areas of the intelligence domain as suggested in "The Business Intelligence System" listing. I have included in this domain the internal organizational environment, which in definitions of the "Business Intelligence" domain, is not included. It seems reasonable to assume that internal information about the organization is part of the universe and the use of "intelligence" that guides corporate planning and decision–making.

6. Among the companies that have participated in war game exercises (and scenarios) as reported in *Business Week,* February 1, 1993, "Oh, What a Lovely War Game," are General Electric, Allied Signal, General Dynamics, Caterpillar, FMC, and Chevron. Some of these corporations are among the handful of U.S. companies that take a relatively serious interest in and commitment to formal intelligence programs.

7. Early in 1993 the National Technical Information Service (NTIS) of the U.S. Department of Commerce and the Japan Informa-

tion Center of Science and Technology extended invitations to businesses and some university professors to attend the Third Annual Joint Conference, which focused on how to acquire Japanese scientific and technical information. This is one example of a government resource that can be utilized.

    8. The former director of the Central Intelligence Agency, Dr. R. M. Gates, in his February 21, 1992 speech to the Oklahoma Press Association indicated that the CIA's Center for the Study of Intelligence would strengthen its outreach program to universities—perhaps those universities listed in the National Intelligence Study Centers survey (see note 4). As of mid-1994, David D. Gries was the director of the center. Sharing CIA economic intelligence with businesses as proposed by CIA Director Woolsey is not enthusiastically supported by all business executives. Some see possible damage to their present international collaborative efforts or fear that their competitors will be the beneficiaries of "intelligence" sharing. Perhaps a way to minimize these misgivings is for the CIA to form a separate "competitive intelligence" office for business. This initiative does not seem too dissimilar to the CIA's venture into the foreign language training software business as reported by *USA Today*, March 15, 1993.

    9. A former government intelligence officer, now in the private sector, has also suggested the need for a dialogue and linkages in a draft position paper prepared in 1993. The position paper has been abstracted as follows, with the author's permission.

A Position on U.S. Government Intelligence Policy Sharing with the Private Sector

The need and practice of business intelligence is growing in importance as American companies face increasing competitive intensity, shorter product life cycles, and an incredibly complex global competitive environment. The cost of ignorance is rising as global competitors strive to outlearn their adversaries and create a sustainable competitive position based on a knowledge edge.

    Recently, the press has reported incidents of foreign espionage operations targeting U.S. firms. These operations are being run by foreign firms as well as by foreign state intelligence organs on behalf of their indigenous firms. Further, ample evidence suggests that the practice is pervasive and growing. It is clear that the ethics and norms under and within which U.S. companies operate are not in effect elsewhere in the world. In fact, a comment credited to a Soviet intelligence defector indicates the basic difference between the U.S. ethic and others: "As long as you persist in making intelligence a moral issue, you will never understand." Representatitves of a number of nations could have made the same statement.

Competitive intensity, environmental complexity, espionage, and a slowing of the world's growth have all contributed to the interest and debate over whether the U.S. government should share intelligence with the private sector. There will be increasing pressure to somehow "even the playing field."

Support for the U.S. government's commitment is needed to guard the very basis for our national competitiveness by proactively countering any attempts to misappropriate U.S. innovations. This means not only in cases where U.S. law has been broken, but also by aggressively raising awareness of all foreign intelligence activity aimed at reducing the competitive position of the United States. The FBI's National Security Threat List (NSTL) program should be fully staffed and supported and advertised for maximum effect. It is believed that any operative definition of national security includes economic security, and therefore, countereconomic espionage and counterindustrial espionage operations are fundamental government responsibilities. Further, support for national trade secret legislation that will provide a basis for a more aggressive counterespionage capability is required.

The complexity associated with the sharing of positive intelligence with the private sector is appreciated. While it is expected that terrorist warnings, health threats, travel warnings, and so on, all examples of intelligence already shared with the private sector, will continue, addressed here is a more narrow class of intelligence—industrial intelligence that would provide value to the efforts of American firms. Issues such as whom to pass intelligence to, whether the firm is American, and can and will the firm protect sensitive information, as well as the threat of possible compromise of sources and methods, are valid concerns and must not be treated lightly. It is believed this area requires more study and broader debate before a satisfactory resolution to some of these dilemmas is possible. Certainly some level of intelligence can be made available, and precedent exists. While not widely known, Foreign Broadcast Information Service (FBIS) is an example of government open source intelligence that is available on a fee basis. Local Commerce Department field offices might consider more regular business intelligence briefings on various subjects as another vehicle for intelligence dissemination. A commission composed of private sector and government members should be formed to generate recommendations covering intelligence content and delivery mechanisms to enhance U.S. competitiveness.

Additionally, the government has the knowledge and capacity to assist American firms in a way that has not received adequate attention. U.S. firms have a duty and obligation to provide their own intelligence and counterintelligence to the best of their abilities. To that end, it is suggested that the government assist the private sector by providing education and training in intelligence disciplines. This assistance would be positive and avoid some of the dilemmas associated with passing intelligence to the private sector. DOD, CIA, and FBI training facilities and cadre could be leveraged to accelerate the private sector's ability to "catch up" with foreign competitors and mitigate a growing knowledge gap.

In conclusion, there is concern about the knowledge-disadvantaged U.S. firm and support for an aggressive defensive posture. Further, it is believed that selected positive intelligence can be made available without compromise and distributed fairly, but this is the most sensitive area and needs a special effort to resolve. Finally, it is believed that the government should consider proposals that will utilize the wealth of knowledge to enhance the capability and competitiveness of U.S. firms.

10. On July 25, 1991, Dr. J. Prescott, then president of SCIP, presented a statement to the Committee on Ways and Means, U.S. House of Representatives: "Factors Affecting U.S. International Competitiveness." He noted that "CI is a tool to help industry make the right decisions, and the U.S. government already has the resources to provide this most important tool."

Conclusion: Reports From the Battlefield

Although little or no substantial research has been undertaken that would help define and identify the CI field, some useful insights have been obtained from field sources. During the past three years, students and faculty in the MBA program course, Competitive Intelligence, at the Hartford Graduate Center have talked with intelligence users and providers at more than twenty-five southern New England corporations. In general, the intent of this small exercise was to find out something about CI programs in these companies— what they are and what they might be if CI were to become a more effective source of competitive advantage. A related objective was to try to identify areas for more formal, systematic, and appropriate research. In the eight mini-case summaries that follow, and in the more than forty conversations, discussions, and interviews that were conducted, six key points emerge that are common both to the majority of the reports and to the focus of this book.

1. Users are not engaged in the process.
2. Much of the CI effort is focused on developing/providing tactical information.

3. CI efforts are informal, not systematic.
4. Provider credibility and information reliability are issues.
5. Analysis is a weakness.
6. Distribution is often ineffective.

The eight summaries are grouped by the major industry in which these companies compete.

LARGE, HIGH-TECH, INDUSTRIAL

- At the present time there is an informal information-gathering effort going on in almost every functional group in the company. The marketing and customer support departments collect considerable information about direct competitors' activities. The bulk of this information is technical product information and provides a current assessment of products presently in the marketplace or which may be close to market entry. The manufacturing departments collect information concerning new equipment, processes, and related information from suppliers and trade associates. Engineering obtains information concerning competing products from their contacts with other manufacturers, engineering associations, government scientific reports, and similar sources. Each department needs some of this information to plan the programs for which it is responsible. At this time there is very little exchange of information between departments. In addition, there is very little perception of the needs of other departments and what value the information that is available might provide. Each information-gathering activity is a stand alone effort operated on a part-time basis by individuals who over time have become "gurus." Someone who has been with the company for a long time gains knowledge of who these gurus are and can search out the expert for advice on specific product questions. Much repetitive information is collected that is never analyzed by anyone. Efforts are put into collecting information that seemingly no one has any use for, even though it is available. There is no systematic sharing or centralized analysis of information that is collected; hence, there is a loss in timeliness and completeness of information used for strategic planning.

- Although there is a focus on research and development, and keeping a step ahead of the competition, there is evidence of a "not invented here" attitude that tends to be skeptical of competitors' plans and operations until they are proven successful. This reactive tendency can result in playing catch-up. Finally, the study of the internal environment seems to be the most reactive. Here, the adage of "if it ain't broke don't fix it" seems to rule. Internal environment investigations seem to be most strongly pursued out of desperation. The good news here, though, is that if we measured the barometer of the reaction to internal environment processes, it would be rising.

LARGE, DIVERSIFIED, INDUSTRIAL

- One thing that is lacking in this company, in addition to a good competitive intelligence department, is a counter-intelligence effort. There does not seem to be any effort or interest in identifying the intelligence-gathering capabilities of competitors.

  A further problem associated with the informal intelligence gathering is that it is deemed sufficient. That is, incomplete or incorrect and unsubstantiated information is often regarded as fact or intelligence. This information is then used to formulate plans and actions; and this often leads to lost time, effort, and investment of resources. Apparently, upper-level management does not see CI as either a differentiated source of actionable information and intelligence or as important to the company. As long as this thinking persists at higher levels, then a good intelligence-gathering system will never be established or operational.

ELECTRONIC, COMPUTER-RELATED SYSTEMS, MEDIUM SIZE

- The current users of this available information are the

finance and marketing departments, using it to mark past and current competitor performance. Performance is measured only in terms of profit/loss or product availability. The available technical data seem also to get only minor use as a "this is how we developed it, this is how they did" mechanism. Again the emphasis is on past competitor performance. The company has a good handle on what the competition has done. Very little attention is placed on what the competition can or will do.

The user/provider relationship at the company is very ambiguous. As stated before, the users do have access to all available information. However, the supply and relative quality of the existing information make demand by users minimal. The providers, with limited experience and resources, cannot answer users' specific questions or spend time trying to get answers. The business intelligence program is in its earliest stage and potential for proper development exists.

OEM INDUSTRIAL COMPONENTS, LARGE

- There are many sources for competitive intelligence in the company. There is a corporate business intelligence staff that tracks and forecasts the key industries and competitors. The business intelligence group is relatively small, consisting of a director/analyst, a collector/analyst, and a clerk. The majority of the effort of this group goes into analyzing the competitive environment and less attention is devoted to individual competitors. Files are maintained on key competitors but analysis is usually only done on a project basis. The BI group publishes bulletins when they detect what they believe to be an important trend or event. They also publish a report annually on the industry trends and projections. This report includes a biography of the key competitors and what actions they have taken over the last year. This report is not widely distributed and many people that could use this intelligence product don't see it.

The business intelligence group is an excellent source of information. The problem with this function is that the information is not disseminated very well. The group is hidden away in a back corner of the corporate building, does not aggressively pursue potential sources for information and is not proactive in disseminating the information. If someone needs the information, they must first know that this group exists and then must try to obtain and assess the value of the information.

FINANCIAL SERVICES, LARGE

- The market, analysis, and research group was organized to do broader, external market scans for higher–level analysis of the local markets. The information was to be used for formulating strategy. Information requests made of this unit, in contrast, have been tactical. The available data from which to draw conclusions has been fragmented. The result has been weakness in analysis.

  The systems problem is being too narrowly focused on maintaining legal conservatism. Threats from new entrants and suppliers who do not have an overt legal interest are overlooked. They have an impact on the regulatory environment that is concerned with cost and delivery of health care. The need is to apply the rest of the health care business to legal concerns when approaching mandates and lobbying.

  Nonlegal units feel hindered in dealing with the legal department which keeps "to the letter of the law." Legal staff sometimes do not have an understanding of what else is going on in the marketplace. Communication becomes frustrating and the intelligence flow is thwarted in such a relationship.

- In the current system, those who obtain a piece of intelligence or read an interesting article have no way of knowing who else may be interested in that information. Things are generally distributed up and down the organizational hierarchy. People don't necessarily know who may have a need for a piece of intelligence unless it's obvious by their job function or through personal knowledge. As a result, not everyone who may have an interest in the intelligence receives it. Distribution is inconsistent and may be significantly delayed.

Part of the problem is that there is no real formal system, just a series of informal data collection services. There are no specific databases on the competition or the environment. Most information is gathered on an ad hoc basis. Any information is fragmented among departmental and functional areas. There is no one source for information. The process, if any, is decentralized. The data is "raw", with no analysis performed.

The six key points or issues that are threaded through these anecdotal observations do not offer any brilliant new insights into the state of CI activity for intelligence providers. They do, however, tend to reinforce the obvious and appropriate concerns among many in the CI industry. These concerns can be distilled into three general questions that have plagued, but have been avoided by, the industry for the past decade: Why does business need a CI function? Why should the business invest in, support, and commit to CI? What are the differential/competitive advantages?

Until the industry players can answer these questions to the satisfaction of senior managers and decision makers—key intelligence users—CI will continue to be adrift in a kind of information no–man's land. To satisfactorily answer the above question(s), we must first know a great deal more about our industry and market. The appendixes suggest what knowledge must be obtained.

Appendix A

Business Intelligence Study Center Survey

Many people in the intelligence industry share concerns about the growth and professionalization of the competitive intelligence function. These concerns include related issues of purpose, domain and management acceptance, support, and utilization of a formal intelligence program. They also recognize that basic and fundamental research about the industry has not yet been developed or undertaken. If we believe that there are impediments to further industry growth that should be recognized and that the related issues are central to the bottleneck problem, then a substantial research effort in appropriate areas is relevant. The industry clearly needs "intelligence" about both supply and demand sides of the industry.

Following a series of meetings and discussions organized in 1991 with intelligence providers and users, Jan Herring and I established the Business Intelligence Study Center (BISC) to facilitate research and to disseminate the results of research initiatives that might be undertaken. This appendix presents an abstract resulting from the first BISC research project: a survey of 330 business organization intelligence providers who were selected from among the approximately 1,800 members of the Society of

Competitive Intelligence Professionals. The three open–ended questions in the survey were intended as a first step to learn something from the intelligence providers perspective about intelligence providers' characteristics
and how they view their intelligence universe. From the 10 percent of the sample that responded, two primary conclusions seem appropriate.

1. The domain of the intelligence program and the important qualifications associated with supply side providers and managers have not been defined or agreed upon. This can, in part, account for the problems and issues related to the intelligence bottleneck—too much (unfocused) supply and too little (user) demand.

2. Further research initiatives concerning both the intelligence supply and demand sides should be undertaken if the intelligence bottleneck is to be cleared.

We would like to acknowledge and thank Gregory Sparzo, who was an MBA candidate at the time the survey was undertaken, and who worked with me and Jan Herring on compiling and organizing the survey results.

Survey Responses and Analysis
BISC Survey 0010
December 1992

Of 330 questionnaires mailed to selected members of the Society of Competitive Intelligence Professionals, 35 responses were received, of which 30 were used to develop this summary. It is important to describe the intent of the questions, along with the results, especially because of the divergent ways in which the questions were answered. Question 1 sought to identify those skills that should be learned or acquired by *both* intelligence managers and intelligence practitioners, while Question 3 attempted to determine which *personal characteristics* were best suited for managers and practitioners of business intelligence. Question 2 was interpreted several ways by respondents. In fact, 13 of 33 responses either did not answer the question or stated that they did not fully understand the question, but attempted to answer to the best of their ability. The intention of Question 2 was to solicit opinions about *the realm* or universe of the intelligence function, that is, what information, systems, disciplines, or sensitivities fall under the heading of competitive intelligence.

Question 1 was divided into skills and characteristics of managers and practitioners. However, the overwhelming majority of respondents made their lists without regard to category. There were forty-six skills/characteristics mentioned by the respondents, twenty-five of them more than once. The most commonly mentioned skill/characteristic was computer and online database searching, with seventeen respondents, followed closely by analytical skills with sixteen respondents. The third most mentioned skill was organizational (nine) tied with writing (nine), then the vaguely descriptive *strategic analysis* and financial analysis skills tied at seven. Research skills, communications skills, and industry experience tied with five. All others resulted in either one or two responses.

In analyzing these responses, the open-ended nature of the questions made it likely that important skills might not be mentioned by a respondent who would almost certainly add a given skill to the list if asked if that particular skill were important. For example, while reading skills were mentioned only by two respondents, one could assume that virtually all intelligence providers and managers would agree that reading skills are important intelligence attributes.

Several skills that might be assumed to be very important were mentioned only once; for example, investigative skills, product knowledge, and common sense were only mentioned by one respondent.

Given the wide-ranging responses to Question 1, and diversity of opinion as to the profile of the ideal intelligence practitioner, it might be concluded that: (1) there is limited experience to draw on; (2) various businesses see things quite differently owing to their particular products, marketing, technology, and so on; and (3) the intelligence field is not yet a well-defined profession.

Question 3 responses, while intended to identify *personal characteristics* as opposed to skills and competencies, closely mirrored Question 1. Respondents did segregate their responses by the manager/practitioner division called for in the question. There were a total of fifty-eight different characteristics mentioned. For *intelligence managers*, the most common personal characteristic mentioned was industry experience, a "skill" that might more appropriately be listed under Question 1, but nonetheless was the most common response to Question 3. Sixteen people included this "characteristic" on their survey. Analytical skill was second with six responses, followed by a three-way tie between experience in information management, an MBA, and creative thinking with five respondents. The fourth most mentioned responses were curiosity, tenacity, and high integrity, all with four responses. It is interesting to note that characteristics that were highly ranked in Question 3 were often barley mentioned in Question 1.[1]

The responses for *intelligence practitioners* closely mirrored those for managers with several exceptions. Industry experience was ranked #1 for practitioners, but with a slightly lower score of fourteen (versus sixteen). The #2 spot was a tie between curiosity and analytical skills with eight responses. There was a tie for third place between creative thinking and an MBA, with a score of six. Other attributes mentioned included highly educated, open-minded, organized, computer-literate, and communication skills, among others.

Question 2 offered a wide, diverse, and divergent range of answers. Many responses summarized aspects of Questions 1 and 3, and a significant number of those who responded to this question mentioned the importance of knowledge of the business environment, governmental policies, competitors, and worldwide market trends. One respondent succinctly observed, "the user/decision-maker role is dominant, all others derive their scope from this primal perspective. There are virtually no limits on the scope and range of interest, knowledge, etc. of the practitioner." This response comes closest to answering the question as it was posed. Many of the answers had a decidedly *supply side* perspective, speaking to areas such as involvement of the salesforce in data gathering, knowledge of finance, and the like, whereas this particular response addresses the demand side of the competitive intelligence equation. Ultimately the domain and scope of interest and knowledge that is important to the business intelligence function should be whatever is relevant to the user's and decision maker's need for information.

An analysis of the responses indicates the major business and industry categories of companies that employed survey respondents.

Of the thirty usable responses, four were from the insurance industry and four were from the telecommunications industry. Other industries represented included banking, automotive components, software, pharmaceuticals, and regulated utilities. It seems reasonable to assume that highly competitive intelligence industries like telecommunications and insurance would have active competitive intelligence functions, but the number of regulated utilities represented in the survey responses is somewhat surprising. However, there is little or no correlation between respondent firms' interest, commitment, or level of development and that of any given firm or industry intelligence function. There were too few responses, and the survey sample of 330 was not categorized by industry.

Another observation concerning the wide variety of responses to the survey questions is that unlike a more clearly defined profession, with a generally accepted body of knowledge and a general agreement as to the boundaries of that profession, competitive intelligence functions seem to cover a wide range of perceptions and practices with no particular common core of skills and competencies. These wide-ranging responses perhaps reflect the uncertainty of the intelligence function itself and the relative newness of the intelligence industry. The industry is only now beginning to acquire some knowledge about itself.

THE INTELLIGENCE PROVIDER

SKILLS-KNOWLEDGE-CHARACTERISTICS
BISC 0010 SURVEY 1992

1. What are the necessary skills and competencies that should be possessed by intelligence managers and practitioners (i.e., what should be learned/acquired)?

THE INTELLIGENCE PROVIDER
(continued)

SKILLS–KNOWLEDGE–CHARACTERISTICS
BISC 0010 SURVEY 1992

2. Define/describe the scope of interest and knowledge (the
    domain) that is important to the intelligence manager and
    practitioner that would contribute to an effective intel-
    ligence system. There may be more than one domain in
    the external/internal organizational environment (i.e.,
    conceptually, the user/decision–maker, the intelligence
    provider, etc.). If so, does it make any difference, and if it
    does, how?

3. What are the necessary personal characteristics of (1) an
    intelligence manager, and (2) an intelligence practitioner
    (i.e., experience, education, personality, etc.)?

Please use the enclosed return envelope for your response.

Optional

           Name   _____

    Organization   _____

                       _____

Table A.1
BISC Survey Responses by Company and Industry

<u>Company</u>	<u>Industry</u>
GM Auto Components Group	Automotive
United Technologies Automotive	Automotive
GM–AC Rochester Div.	Automotive
Royal Bank of Canada	Banking
FMC Corporation	Chemicals
Electronic Data Systems	Computer Services
Control Data Corporation	Computers
PRC Inc.	Consulting
Texas Instruments	Electronics
Westinghouse Electric Corp.	Electronics
Aetna Life & Casualty	Insurance
Mass. Mutual Life	Insurance
Physicians Mutual Insurance	Insurance
UNUM Life Insurance	Insurance
Xerox	Office Equipment
Polaroid	Optical
S. D. Warren	Paper Mfg.
Phillips Petroleum Company	Petroleum
Bristol–Myers Squibb	Pharmaceuticals
SmithKline Beecham	Pharmaceuticals
GTE Directories	Publishing
Standard & Poors Info. Group	Publishing
Johnson Controls	Rubber Products
3M	Scientific & Photographic
BMC Software	Software
Northern Telecom	Telecommunications
NYNEX	Telecommunications
Pacific Bell	Telecommunications
Southwestern Bell	Telecommunications
Louisville Gas & Electric	Utilities

Table A.2
BISC Survey Responses Question 1

Score	Skills and Competencies
16	Analytical Skills
16	Computers, Online Database
9	Organizational Skills
9	Writing Skills
7	Strategic Analysis Skills
7	Financial Skills
6	Presentation Skills
6	Research Skills
5	Communication Skills
5	Industry Experience
4	Resourceful
3	Business Analysis
3	Interpersonal Skills
3	Ethical Skills
3	Statistical Analysis Skills
2	Time Management Skills
2	Detail Oriented
2	Creative
2	Interview Skills
2	Marketing Skills
2	Customer Focus
2	Ear of Management
2	Reading Skills
2	Decision–Making Skills
2	Common Sense
1	Curiosity
1	Enthusiasm
1	Problem–Solving Skills
1	Product Knowledge
1	MBA

Table A.2 continued

BISC Survey Responses Question 1

Score	Skills and Competencies
1	Relationship Development
1	Proactive
1	Investigative Skills
1	Project Management Skills
1	Logical Skills
1	Ability to Deal with Contradictions
1	Listening Skills
1	Marketing Skills
1	Negotiation Skills
1	Networking Skills

Table A.3

BISC Survey Responses Question 3

Score	Skills and Competencies
16	Industry Experience
6	Analytical Skills
5	Experience with Information Mgt.
5	MBA
5	Creative Thinking
5	Highly Educated
4	Curiosity
4	Relationship Development
4	Tenacious/Persistent
4	High Integrity and Principles
4	Engaging Personality
3	Communication Skills
3	Organized

Table A.3 continued

BISC Survey Responses Question 3	
<u>Score</u>	**Skills and Competencies**
3	Credibility
2	Generalist
2	Good Listener
2	Patience
2	Computer–Literate
2	Intuitive
1	Contacts
1	Financial Skills
1	Motivation
1	Team Player
1	Science Background
1	Access to Senior Management
1	Think Outside the Box
1	Problem–Solving Skills
1	Dedication to the Team
1	Willingness to Learn
1	Political Acuity
1	Competitive Personality
1	Accessible
1	Attention to Detail
1	Fast Reader
1	Intelligence
1	Presentation Skills
1	Logical
1	Liberal Arts Background
1	Military Intelligence Experience
1	Nosey
1	Experience as a Provider
1	Group Facilitator

Table A.3 continued

BISC Survey Responses Question 3	
<u>Score</u>	**Skills and Competencies**
1	Leadership Skills
1	Extraversion, Intuition Thinking, Perception (Myers–Briggs)
1	Marketing Skills
1	Strategic Thinker
1	Phone Skills
1	Conceptual Acuity

Table A.4

BISC Survey Responses Question 3	
<u>Score</u>	**Skills and Competencies**
14	Industry Experience
8	Analytical Skills
8	Curiosity
6	MBA
6	Creative Thinking
5	Highly Educated
4	Tenacious/Persistent
4	High Integrity and Principles
4	Engaging Personality
4	Organized
3	Experience with Information Management
3	Open–Minded
3	Communication Skills
3	Computer–Literate

Table A.4 continued

BISC Survey Responses Question 3	
<u>Score</u>	**Skills and Competencies**
2	Generalist
2	Good Listener
2	Intuitive
2	Motivated
2	Problem–Solving Skills
2	Nosey
2	Intelligent
2	Presentation Skills
1	Credibility
1	Contacts
1	Financial Skills
1	Motivation
1	Think Outside the Box
1	Dedication to the Team
1	Willingness to Learn
1	Political Acuity
1	Conceptual Acuity
1	Competitive Personality
1	Accessible
1	Attention to Detail
1	Fast Reader
1	Logical
1	Liberal Arts Background
1	Introversion, Intuition Thinking, Perception (Myers–Briggs)
1	Marketing Skills
1	Strategic Thinker
1	Phone Skills
1	Detail–Oriented

NOTE

1. Jan P. Herring of the Futures Group lists the following as desirable characteristics of BI/CI managers: leadership, diplomacy management, educator, writer and orator, salesperson and marketer, and ethical advocate. Don E. Colmenares of Phillips Petroleum Company suggests that the BI/CI manager should possess the following skills and qualities: ability to cultivate sponsorship and networking, credibility with top management, salesmanship and communication skills, broad business knowledge, risk-taker/ challenges norm, and information technology user. These listings were included in presentations by Herring and Colmenares at the 1993 SCIP annual conference. John C. Reichenback, Jr. of PPG Industries, at the same conference, listed the following as important skills and attitudes that should be possessed by the intelligence director: critical skills—synthesis, analysis, logic, objectivity, experience, flexibility, technical knowledge, communications/networking, social and teaching, attitudes—curiosity, credibility, extrovert, persistent, detail, relational, and courageous.

Appendix B

CI Research and Research Issues

Research that would help characterize the CI industry, the position of CI in the competitive information industry, and the application of a CI process and resultant products, essentially has been nonexistent. The lack of usable and useful "intelligence" about the industry is largely due to the fact that the industry—its scope and domain, terminology, purpose, its members, and its market—has yet to be defined. There should be some common and agreed–upon boundaries that can serve to identify a purpose and focus for research and inquiry. Without some reasonable agreement on the nature of the universe to be explored, it is enormously difficult and inefficient to determine what usefully should be measured, why, and how. Without some definition, it is not possible to formulate and test assumptions, theories, and applications, and to establish appropriate measures to test and evaluate observations.

However, there is a positive side of sorts to the present condition of an undefined CI industry. It has allowed and encouraged some academics, consultants, and research firms to select anything to research or survey from the infinite possibilities of factors and elements that may serve some individual or organizational interest or purpose. These interests and purposes can range from doctoral dissertations on how CI influences strategic decisions to consultant/ researcher presentations before various information association and society audiences on the annual budget for CI operations in European textile businesses. There are some possible benefits to all this random and often variously focused effort. It is often entertaining, sometimes published in association journals, and occasionally relevant to the interests of a few intelligence providers or vendors who attend the conferences or read the journals. A possible future benefit may also be derived from some of the surveys and research when the CI industry is more universally understood and defined. It isn't possible now to know if there will be any value in the future to the past and present research initiatives. From what follows, the reader may be able to discern some present or future benefit. What follows are two research–related topics.

First, in Part 1, is a partial listing of research and survey initiatives that have been undertaken within the past few years. The focus is on the supply side—providers and various provider support systems—which does little if anything to suggest issues, impediments, and problems on the demand side that sorely need attention. Further, there is no standard against which to relate much of the information, or indeed to determine the reliability of responses to the research inquiry and the meaning and credibility of the results.

Part 2 explores some of the necessary research initiatives and how they might be implemented.

APPENDIX B—PART 1
Past and Current CI Research/Survey Initiatives

The listing that follows does not, in all probability, represent the entire universe of research initiatives in the CI field. The listing represents only those projects that have been identified through the title or purpose with CI. Excluded are initiatives that relate to the general universe of information or information systems. The list has been developed with assistance from various academics, consultants, SCIP, and my own CI resource sources. The various initiatives are roughly grouped according to content or purpose (i.e., provider information, system/organization) and are identified by title, author or initiator, purpose, scope, methodology, results or determinations (if any), and dates of the initiative. If the survey or research is known to have been published, I also indicate the publication.

Research/Survey Initiatives

A. Provider Information

  1. 1993 SIS Global CI Survey

     • Ruth Stanat, SIS International

     • Providers; also organization/networks

     • Ten thousand questionnaires to marketing, market research, strategic planning, and information managers/providers. 4.5 percent response rate. Seventeen industries represented in sample.

     • Statistical tabulation of results.

     • January–March 1993.

  2. "The View—A Survey of SCIP's VIP's." *Competitive Intelligence Review*, vol. 4, no.1, Spring 1993, pp. 33–37, as reported in the *CIR* issue. The survey was mailed in January 1993 to information professionals (225) listed in the SCIP membership directory. The survey was intended to describe salaries, degrees, value–added products and services, and titles among this group.

  3. "SCIP: Who We Are, What We Do." *Competitive Intelligence Review*, vol. 2, no. 1, Spring 1991. A survey of the SCIP membership covering background information, organizational CI background, CI unit mission, sources of competititve intelligence, types of intelligence monitored, and dissemination of CI.

B. CI Relationships to Corporate Strategy/Planning

  1. 1991 Cambridge Strategic Management Group (CSMG) *proposal* for survey/questionnaire of twenty–five U.S. companies. Response to SCIP Request for Proposal (RFP)

- Claudia L. Hanlin

- Providers

2. 1991 FIND/SVP *proposal* for survey/interviews of fifty U.S. companies. Response to SCIP RFP.

- Timothy W. Powell, Research Director

- Providers

3. 1991 SIS International *proposal* for survey/questionnaire of ten U.S. and non–U.S. firms to determine best/worst case practices of integrating CI and strategic planning. Response to SCIP RFP.

- Ruth Stanat, President

- Providers

The preliminary Jaworski/Chee Wee survey findings (and methodology) were reported in the *Competitive Intelligence Review,* vol. 3, no. 3/4, Fall 1992/Winter 1993. (See Chapter 1, note 8.)

C. CI Processes

1. 1993 case study of ten Swedish companies to determine BI organization/processes/problems.

- Department of Business Administration, School of Economics and Management, Lund University. Hans Hedin. Doctoral candidate. Dissertation proposal.

- Providers. Survey/interviews.

- Results presented at annual Association of Global Strategic Information conference, June 1993.

2. Survey of business intelligence practices, 1992

- Benn Kansynski, Research Fellow, Harvard Business School.

- Two surveys. Directors of BI and CEOs' attitudes, practices, ethics.

APPENDIX B—PART 2
Further Research Initiatives For the CI Industry

There are perhaps five generic areas of inquiry or research that would be useful for the CI industry to address in the very near future. These research areas would serve two important purposes:

1. Assist understanding and knowledge of the industry
2. Serve to further develop and refine programs, plans, and actions that will benefit and strengthen the CI industry and CI's position in the information industry

The suggested generic study areas are:

- intelligence users/customers
- industry characteristics
- training and development of CI providers
- SCIP membership characteristics
- CI functional competition

These research areas may be initiated and implemented in a number of ways, such as through

- SCIP
- academic/graduate schools of management
- outside consulting/research firms
- others (i.e., conference board, government agencies)

Which approach may be appropriate for a given area might be evaluated in terms of a matrix:

Vehicle

Research Area	SCIP	Academe	Business	Other
• Intelligence users		X		X
• Industry			X	X
• Training	X	X		X
• SCIP	X			
• CI competitors		X		X

For example, intelligence users' research would seek to identify reasons/impediments as to why senior management/key decision-makers do not support CI. Is it because they have other, more traditional, credible, usable sources of information? Have negative views of CI? Cannot differentiate CI from other "intelligence" systems or programs? Other? Further, it would be useful to know more precisely what is meant by "intelligence user." Who are the users? What is the CI customer market? How do these customers make decisions, the process/what kinds of decisions (long- or short-term) when/where/why? This "demand side" intelligence is currently not available to assist industry efforts to professionalize and legitimize CI. A research project or projects in this area may be of interest to appropriate academics, the conference board, or an educational/management foundation.

The four other suggested areas for research might provide specific research topics, such as:

The Industry
- What is the CI industry?
- Who are the players/stakeholders?
- What is the CI domain/universe?
- What terminology is appropriate (i.e., BI or CI) and acceptable to CI customers?

Provider Training
- What skills/competencies/attributes are important?
- How can they be acquired/learned/taught?
- Who (business/government/academe) should provide training?
- Is provider skill/"professionalism" an issue in concerns about provider credibility and reliability?

SCIP (and perhaps further insight into industry characteristics)
- Members/membership 1986–present
- The numbers: number new joined/number left/number retained from previous year(s)

	New	Old	Left

- who (by internal function
  or some classification)

- why

- conference attendees

Competition

- What information systems (formal and informal) are CI
  competitors?

- How are they positioned?

- Are they differentiated in some way, and do they serve
  particular segments of the information user market?

If there is one question to be answered that is common to each of these five research initiatives, it is this: Why do businesses need CI? This question is significant as it has to do with the related question of what does or should differentiate CI as the intelligence system of choice for users and, thus, how CI is to be defined, described and characterized to make it the "intelligent" choice of intelligence users.

Selected Bibliography

Barndt, W. D. "Linking Competitive Intelligence to Competitiveness." *Competitive Intelligence Review*, vol. 3, no. 2, Summer 1992, 26–30.

Barndt, W. D. "The Intelligence Bottleneck: Too Much Supply, Too Little Demand." *Journal of the Association for Global Strategic Information*, vol. 2, issue 2, July 1993, 86–99.

Crockett, F. "Revitalizing Executive Information Systems." *Sloan Management Review.* Summer 1992, 39–47.

Fuld, Leonard. 1985. *Competitive Intelligence.* New York: Wiley.

Ghashal, J., and D. E. Westney "Organizing Competitor Analysis Systems." *Strategic Management Journal,* vol 12, 1991, 17–31.

Gilad, B. and T. 1988. *The Business Intelligence System.* New York: AMACOM.

Herring, J. P. "Senior Management Must Champion Business Intelligence Programs." *Journal of Business Strategy,* September–October 1991.

Jacobsen, R. "The Austrian School of Strategy." *Academy of Management Review,* vol. 17, no. 4, 1992, 782–807.

Kennedy, P. 1993. *Preparing for the Twenty–First Century.* New York: Random House.

Magaziner, I. and M. Patinkin 1989. *The Silent War.* New York: Random House.

Meyer, H. E. 1987. *Real World Intelligence: Organized Information for Executives.* New York: Weidenfeld and Nicolson.

O'Toole, G. J. H. 1991. "Honorable Treachery." *Atlantic Monthly Press.*

Pfaff, William. "Perils of Policy". *Harpers Magazine,* May 1987.

Pitts, R. A., and G. C. Snow. 1986. *Strategies for Competitive Success.* New York: Wiley.

Porter, M. E. 1980. *Competitive Strategy.* New York: Macmillan (The Free Press).

Prescott, J. E., and P. T. Gibbons. 1993. "Global Perspectives on Competitive Intelligence." Washington, D.C.: Society of Competitive Intelligence Professionals.

Prescott, J. E., and D. C. Smith. "The Largest Survey of Leading Edge Competitor Intelligence Managers." *Planning Review,* May-June 1989, 6–13.

Rothschild, William E. 1989. *How to Gain and Maintain the Competitive Advantage in Business.* New York: McGraw-Hill.

Shulsky, A. N. 1991. *Silent Warfare.* McLean: Brassey's (U.S.).

Sohweizer, Peter. 1993. "Friendly Spies". New York: *Atlantic Monthly Press.*

Winks, Robin W. 1989. *Cloak and Gown: Scholars in the Secret War.* New York: Morrow.

Index

About the Author and Contributors

Walter D. Barndt, Jr. is Professor of Management at The Hartford Graduate Center. Since 1983, he has taught the only continuous competitive intelligence course in a U.S. graduate school management program. He serves as a director of The Society of Competitive Intelligence Professionals and has published recent articles in The Competitive Intelligence Review, The Journal of the Association of Global Strategic Information and The Journal of Business Strategy.

CONTRIBUTORS

Jan P. Herring is Vice President for Business Intelligence and Strategy at The Futures Group. Subsequent to a twenty-year career with the Central Intelligence Agency, he established the first formal business intelligence program in the U.S. at Motorola in 1984. His articles have appeared in The Journal of Business Strategy, CEO magazine and The Competitive Intelligence Review.

Marshall N. Heyman, Ph.D. is the founder and director of The Behavioral Assessment Systems Center. He retired from the Central Intelligence Agency as Chief Psychologist for Operational support in 1979. He continues to consult on national security matters with various government agencies and has published articles in Behavioral Sciences and the Law, Police Chief magazine, and Personality Assessment System Foundation Journal.

ISBN 0-89930-781-7

EAN

HARDCOVER BAR CODE